Going Viral

WORLD BANK LATIN AMERICAN AND CARIBBEAN STUDIES

Going Viral: COVID-19 and the Accelerated Transformation of Jobs in Latin America and the Caribbean

Guillermo Beylis, Roberto Fattal Jaef, Michael Morris, Ashwini Rekha Sebastian, and Rishabh Sinha

Contents

Foreword

Latin America and the Caribbean is the region most affected by the COVID-19 pandemic, with health and economic challenges as large as those in advanced economies but without the necessary resources to protect employment and sustain economic activity. It is a complex and painful scenario in which millions are suffering through the huge daily challenges facing the region and the devastating consequences for their jobs and earnings.

In addition to the new challenges that the pandemic and the policy response to it have posed, the current crisis has, sadly, exposed and deepened some of the old problems the region was already facing. A segmented labor market and social protection system have been able to protect the jobs and earnings of formal workers while leaving many informal workers unprotected and facing the dire choice of confronting health risks or being unable to sustain their families.

In *Going Viral: COVID-19 and the Accelerated Transformation of Jobs in Latin America and the Caribbean*, the authors dig into the underlying trends that were transforming the labor market even before the pandemic. Unfortunately, the current economic crisis associated with the pandemic has only accelerated these trends, bringing the region nearer to the future and consequently making the policy reforms needed to help create more and better jobs even more urgent.

More vibrant job creation requires overcoming the region's chronically low levels of productivity growth. This will demand investments in smart infrastructure, adoption of new technologies, promotion of competition and product upgrading, and removal of market distortions that impede the growth of the most productive firms. Also, the region would benefit from increasing international trade not only in goods but, perhaps more importantly, in services. The enormous potential of Latin America and the Caribbean will only materialize if the right policies are put in place.

At the same time, the region needs to invest in the human capital of its workforce. The jobs of the future will require a very different skill set, especially when compared with that needed in the many informal jobs available at present. Countries have to prepare their children and teenagers by investing now in schools and universities and by improving the learning content of education. But countries also need to adopt retraining and job placement programs for adults who have seen their jobs disappear.

Finally, the region must rethink its labor regulations and social protection systems so that they promote the creation of jobs while encouraging the formalization of workers. The region is already plagued with high informality and with trends indicating a future of work that involves more freelancing and independent workers; new regulations must not only help create new jobs but also expand the benefits of social protection to larger segments of the workforce.

Perhaps one of the greatest challenges for Latin America and the Caribbean will be the creation of new and better jobs in the context of shifting sectoral employment and technological evolution. The huge economic and social costs created by the pandemic have accelerated the transformation of jobs and make the challenge more urgent than ever. But inclusion through better jobs is unavoidable if we want more equal societies. That will be the key measure of success.

Carlos Felipe Jaramillo
Regional Vice President for Latin America
and the Caribbean
World Bank

Acknowledgments

This book was prepared by a team led by Guillermo Beylis. The core team also consisted of Roberto Fattal Jaef, Michael Morris, Ashwini Rekha Sebastian, and Rishabh Sinha. The team received excellent research assistance from Julian Eduardo Diaz Gutierrez and Maria Ignacia Paz Cuevas de Saint Pierre. The work was conducted under the general guidance of Carlos Végh, former Chief Economist for the Latin America and the Caribbean (LAC) region of the World Bank, and Martin Rama, current Chief Economist for the LAC region, with substantial inputs from Daniel Lederman, former LAC Deputy Chief Economist, and Elena Ianchovichina, current LAC Deputy Chief Economist.

Background papers were prepared by Guillermo Beylis, Julian Eduardo Diaz Gutierrez, Roberto Fattal Jaef, Steven Helfand, Maria Ignacia Paz Cuevas de Saint Pierre, and Rishabh Sinha. We are very grateful for their original and outstanding contributions, as well as the many insightful conversations with them.

The team was fortunate to receive excellent advice and guidance from three distinguished peer reviewers: Jorge Araujo, Ernesto López-Córdova, and Richard Rogerson. Although the team is very grateful for the guidance received, these reviewers are not responsible for any remaining errors, omissions, or interpretations. Additional insights from Rita Almeida, Samuel Pienknagura, Marc Schiffbauer, Francisco Carneiro, Óscar Calvo-González, and other participants in a workshop held on April 3, 2018, are gratefully acknowledged.

Sabra Ledent was the editor. Patricia Katayama (acquisitions editor), Mary Fisk (production editor), and Orlando Mota (print coordinator) of the World Bank's formal publishing program were responsible for managing the editing, design, typesetting, and printing of the book. Last, but not least, the authors thank Ruth Eunice Flores and Jacqueline Larrabure for superb administrative support.

About the Authors

Guillermo Beylis is a research economist in the Office of the Chief Economist, Latin America and the Caribbean, at the World Bank. He specializes in labor markets, with a focus on skills, gender, and inequality. He has published on many different topics, including energy, international capital flows, inequality, and skills. He holds an MA and a PhD in economics from the University of California, Los Angeles (UCLA), and a BA and an MA from the University Torcuato di Tella, Buenos Aires, Argentina.

Roberto Fattal Jaef is an economist with the Macroeconomics and Growth Team of the World Bank's Development Research Group. His research interests include various areas of macroeconomics, with a special emphasis on economic growth. He has published in leading journals such as the *American Economic Journal: Macroeconomics*, *Journal of Development Economics*, and *Journal of International Economics*. Prior to joining the World Bank, he worked in the International Monetary Fund's Research Department. He holds a PhD in economics from UCLA.

Michael Morris is a lead agriculture economist with the World Bank, currently mapped to the Latin America and the Caribbean region. He conducts research and is involved in the preparation, implementation, and evaluation of lending operations. His areas of expertise include agricultural policy, marketing systems and value chain development, and agricultural innovation systems. Before joining the World Bank, he spent 16 years with the Mexico-based International Maize and Wheat Improvement Center (CIMMYT). He holds a BA from Amherst College and an MSc and a PhD from Michigan State University.

Ashwini Rekha Sebastian is an economist at the World Bank, currently mapped to the Latin America and the Caribbean region. There she works on themes related to agriculture and food systems, environmental conservation, rural livelihoods, jobs, and poverty reduction. Prior to joining the World Bank, she worked as an economist in the United Nations Food and Agriculture Organization's Economic and Social Development Division on the Protection to Production team. She previously collaborated with the International Food Policy Research Institute, including on research related to environmental migration and labor market integration. Ashwini holds a BA in economics and mathematics from

Bryn Mawr College, as well as an MSc and a PhD in agricultural and natural resource economics and an MSc in economics from the University of Maryland, College Park.

Rishabh Sinha is an economist with the Macroeconomics and Growth Team of the World Bank's Development Research Group. His interests lie in understanding the role of allocative efficiency in delivering economic growth. He has studied this relationship in diverse settings, which include issues involving structural transformation, occupational choice, financial development, intergenerational mobility, and fragile and violent economies. Before joining the World Bank in 2015, Rishabh worked at the Federal Reserve Bank of Kansas City and in the private financial sector. He holds an MS in economics from the Indian Statistical Institute (Kolkata) and an MS and a PhD in economics from Arizona State University.

Abbreviations

AI	artificial intelligence
ATM	automated teller machine
CEDLAS	Center for Distributive, Labor and Social Studies (Universidad de la Plata in Argentina)
DOT	Dictionary of Occupational Titles
ENHRUM	Mexico National Rural Household Survey
FDI	foreign direct investment
GDP	gross domestic product
GGDC	Groningen Growth and Development Centre
GVC	global value chain
ICT	information and communications technology
IoT	Internet of Things
ISCO	International Standard Classification of Occupations
LAC	Latin America and the Caribbean
MxFLS	Mexican Family Life Survey
NR-CA	nonroutine cognitive analytical
NR-CP	nonroutine cognitive interpersonal
NR-MP	nonroutine manual physical
OECD	Organisation for Economic Co-operation and Development
O*NET	Occupational Information Network
PIACC	Programme for the International Assessment of Adult Competencies
PPP	purchasing power parity

PtoP	Protection to Production
R&D	research and development
RBTC	routine-biased technological change
RC	routine cognitive
RM	routine manual
RoW	rest of world
SBTC	skill-biased technological change
SEDLAC	Center for Distributive, Labor and Social Studies (Universidad de la Plata in Argentina)
SOC	Standard Occupational Classification
STEP	Skills Toward Employability and Productivity
TFP	total factor productivity

Introduction

COVID-19 started as a health emergency, but it is rapidly evolving into an employment crisis. The year 2020 could well witness the biggest contraction in economic activity that the region has experienced since the Great Depression. Lower external demand; a protracted period of quarantines and lockdowns; short-term liquidity constraints evolving into solvency problems for firms; and in some cases, financial crises are undermining the demand for labor and putting an increasingly large number of jobs at risk. The limited fiscal space enjoyed by many countries in the region also makes it difficult for governments to support economic activity. There is still uncertainty about how severe the economic impact of the pandemic will be. However, the drag on the region's employment could last longer than the epidemic itself.

The COVID-19 crisis is affecting not only the level of employment but also its composition. Different sectors of activity have been impacted by quarantines and lockdowns to different extents. Services that could be delivered electronically have held well, or even thrived, while sectors that require human contact to be provided have struggled the most. The consequences have also differed by type of job. Formal sector workers, who get a paycheck at the end of the month, can be more easily reached by social protection programs than informal sector workers, who make their living on a daily basis. Some of these differential effects may recede as the epidemic is contained, but others may have long-lasting effects.

These changes in the level and composition of employment are taking place in a region that was already undergoing a significant transformation of its labor markets. For a long time, the hope was that Latin America and the Caribbean would become a more industrial region, one where wage employment and formality would be increasingly prevalent. Instead, the actual trends have included premature deindustrialization, a plateauing level of formality, and a steady growth of independent work.

Globalization and technology lagged behind this transformation in the employment structure of the region, leading to the expectation that the trends would continue over time. The COVID-19 crisis, however, could actually accelerate them, bringing the future much closer than anticipated and possibly calling for new and better-adapted economic policies. Understanding what to expect, and how to react, requires a deep grasp of the underlying trends and the ways in which they may be amplified in the coming years. This report analyzes how the economic structure of the region has evolved in recent years and how this transformation is affecting both productivity growth and the nature of jobs.

Following the so-called Golden Decade (2003–13) of rapid development and strong improvements in social indicators, economic growth had stalled across most of Latin America and the Caribbean. In the few years preceding the COVID-19 crisis, the external environment no longer provided tailwinds to foster an economic rebound. Foreign direct investment had moderated, trade had slowed amid elevated geopolitical tensions, and commodity prices were mostly flat. The region needed to find internal sources of growth and focus on a productivity-enhancing reform agenda. That need is even more urgent today, as the region struggles with the consequences of the pandemic and the dramatic lockdown measures that many countries adopted to contain it.

Although increasing productivity may sound like an abstract concept, it translates in practice into creating more and better jobs. In Latin America and the Caribbean, the year preceding the COVID-19 outbreak was a time of intense social unrest. In a dozen countries, discontent led to violence, leaving large numbers of people dead or wounded. It is difficult to attribute this unrest to any single factor, whether economic, social, or institutional. Political circumstances specific to each country certainly played a role. Yet a frustration over unmet expectations seems to cut across many of the episodes. In this context, a disappointing employment performance can only be a cause for concern.

Analyzing structural transformation

As a starting point to understand the ongoing changes in employment, the report focuses on structural transformation, analyzing its drivers and documenting the experience of the region.[1] A well-known stylized fact is that the importance of agriculture in the economy declines with the level of development, both in terms of employment and value-added shares; it declines with the level of development while that of the service sector increases. Perhaps less well-known is the fact that the industrial sector follows a "hump shape" or inverted-U pattern, initially growing at lower levels of GDP per capita during the industrialization phase and then declining at higher levels of income during the deindustrialization phase.

This report focuses on the premature deindustrialization experienced by Latin America and the Caribbean. As shown by Rodrik (2016), developing economies are entering the deindustrialization phase at lower levels of income per capita, and they are achieving lower peaks of industrial shares relative to developed countries. This is concerning, because in most countries the industrial sector has the highest level of labor productivity and the highest rate of productivity growth. When premature deindustrialization occurs, labor moves away from the industrial sector into lower productivity growth sectors—usually services—reducing overall productivity, with negative consequences for real income growth and standards of living.[2] Countries in Latin America and the Caribbean may actually be at the forefront of this process.

Three notable features emerge from this analysis.[3] First, there is substantial heterogeneity across the countries in our sample. The more developed economies, Argentina and Chile, have been deindustrializing for decades. Countries such as Brazil, Colombia, and Mexico display stagnant or slight increases in their industrial employment shares; the least developed nation in our sample, Bolivia, is still industrializing. Second, the deindustrialization process is more pronounced in terms of employment shares than in value-added shares. Third, premature deindustrialization does not necessarily imply a contraction of the industrial sector; the absolute number of jobs in the industrial sector—as opposed to the share of jobs—has been fairly stable or even growing.

The story of deindustrialization in Latin America and the Caribbean is thus not one of factory closures and mass layoffs. Rather, it is a story of a stunted industrialization process whereby the industrial sector has been unable to grow and create jobs over time as it did in today's developed economies. In part, this may be related to the history behind the industrialization phase in the region. Most countries started the industrialization process under the banner of old-school industrial policies of protectionism and subsidies. As globalization took hold, this mostly sheltered industrial sector did not, for the most part, successfully integrate into global value chains. As a result, the industrial sector was unable to grow, limited by the size of domestic and regional markets.

An important question is whether the observed pattern of deindustrialization results from distortions and inefficiencies in the economy, or whether it rather represents an efficient reallocation of resources given the circumstances. Answering this question requires defining an efficient benchmark against which to assess the observed patterns in the data. A standard model of structural transformation is used to this effect. The results show that the deindustrialization of the region that started in the 1980s was inefficient. The implied output loss was modest, but there appear to be significant distortions in the sector, as reflected in a skewed firm size distribution—with firms in the region remaining small by international standards. This finding highlights the importance of revising policies that may be discouraging the growth of firms and incentivizing informality.

Confronting the region is a future in which the service sector will continue to grow and be the main source of job creation. The emergence of new labor-saving technologies in the manufacturing sector will only deepen and accelerate this trend. At the same time, the COVID-19 crisis highlights the heterogeneity of this sector, offering encouraging growth prospects to activities that can operate remotely, while threatening those that depend heavily on personal contact. The latter could still come back if a vaccine or an effective treatment is found. However, the boost for the former could be more permanent, regardless of how the pandemic evolves.

Given this centrality of the services sector, the report calls attention to the complex role it plays in relation to productivity, value added, and job creation. At the aggregate level, the service sector displays lower productivity growth than the industrial sector. Yet the sector is composed of a very diverse set of subsectors that differ significantly in their productivity levels and growth rates—and even in their use of skilled labor. In many countries, some service subsectors—such as telecommunications, finance, and logistics—are more productive and skill intensive than manufacturing and are increasingly sharing pro-development characteristics that were once thought of as unique to manufacturing.

Rapid advances in information and communications technologies, and their accelerated adoption in the aftermath of the COVID-19 crisis, enable the emergence of service sectors that are no longer limited by market size. More and more services can be digitally stored, codified, and easily traded (Ghani and Kharas 2010). Meanwhile, in the years preceding the epidemic outbreak, the deregulation of services markets was accompanied by large inflows of foreign direct investment. Therefore, certain service subsectors were increasingly resembling the manufacturing sector, with exposure to trade and capital flows, allowing for greater competition, technology diffusion, and the benefits of scale.

Importantly, many of these services are emerging as key inputs into industrial and agricultural processes, with numerous forward linkages to other sectors and substantial potential to improve aggregate productivity. New evidence is emerging pointing to a "servicification" of the manufacturing sector. This refers to the phenomenon where manufacturing is increasing the share of services as inputs to the production process (embodied services), as well as offering more sales and after-sales services that are bundled with the sales of goods (embedded services).

The traditional perspective of analyzing and devising policies for each sector independently therefore is becoming increasingly obsolete. The analyses in this report show that reducing distortions in the intermediate market for services could have an important impact on the size of the industrial sector. If distortions in the service market were reduced to their historical minimum, the employment share of the industrial sector could increase by 2 to 3.5 percentage points.

The occupational structure is also changing *within* broad economic sectors. The importance of service occupations is increasing in *all* sectors of the economy. This is clearly related to the servicification of manufacturing phenomenon described, but it extends beyond manufacturing. Market competition and new technologies leverage the contribution of workers who produce intangible value added, such as researchers, marketers, managers, and designers. By favoring telework over personal interaction, the COVID-19 epidemic is bound to further increase the leverage of this group.

As machines replace humans in carrying out simpler, more routine tasks, and the internet replaces personal interaction, workers will have to adapt. They will need to learn how to operate through electronic platforms and devote more of their work time to the more complex, higher-order tasks that are harder to automate and that complement the tasks performed by machines. These rely on cognitive or analytical skills (such as critical thinking, creativity, and problem-solving), as well as interpersonal skills (such as teamwork, negotiation, and management). The report shows that even before the COVID-19 crisis, there was a fall in the demand for routine manual tasks and a rise in the demand for non-routine tasks. The trend is bound to accelerate as remote working becomes more prevalent.

The report evaluates the potential number of jobs that are at high risk of being automated in the region and concludes that fears of mass "technological unemployment" are largely unfounded. Estimates vary widely, however, depending on the methodology used. Many occupations will be affected and transformed by the emerging technologies. Although the overall number of jobs may not fall dramatically, the trend could be accelerated by the social distancing practices the COVID-19 epidemic may foster. Importantly, these future jobs and tasks will require different and higher-order capabilities and skills.

Implications for economic policy

The findings of this report have several important implications for economic policy. Some of these implications are related to the productivity challenges that Latin America and the Caribbean was already facing after the end of the Golden Decade. If anything, the social unrest that emerged across the region in 2019 was a warning that restoring economic growth and fostering the emergence of more and better jobs were urgent priorities. Other policy implications could see their relevance enhanced by the COVID-19 crisis. As sectors are impacted in different ways and working remotely becomes more common, governments need to respond in ways that support a smooth transformation of jobs, one that is socially acceptable and that contributes to productivity growth.

Promoting productivity growth

A first important message of the report is that policy makers should not focus on sectoral size but rather on productivity growth. The emergence of new technologies—under the banner of the Fourth Industrial Revolution—suggests that opportunities for further industrialization (or reindustrialization) are likely to be limited in many developing countries. Requirements in terms of the skills mix and the use of electronic platforms will increase, but these changes tend to be labor-saving. Overall, the industrial sector could continue contributing positively to aggregate productivity growth and value added but not as much to job creation, especially for unskilled labor.

Rather than focusing on sector-specific policies, it will be increasingly relevant to formulate value chain policies that take into account how sectors interact with each other. The servicification of economic activity in general, and of manufacturing in particular, offers new opportunities for growth. Already the largest employer in the region with over 60 percent of the workforce, the services sector is expected to grow even further and play an increasingly crucial role as an input provider to the larger economy. This calls for a comprehensive set of service sector–oriented policies, with an emphasis on the distortions that prevent competition and innovation from occurring at a rapid pace.

Investing in human capital

Second, as new technologies are developed and adopted, and as remote working becomes more prevalent, investing in the human capital of the workforce should be a priority for policy makers. It is no exaggeration to say that education offers the best insurance against the risks of automation (World Bank 2019). It is the low-paid and uneducated workers who are performing the simpler, more routine tasks that are at highest risk of eventually being replaced by machines. The same is true of the workers in high-contact activities, such as those characterizing the informal sector of the economy.

In recent decades, countries in Latin America and the Caribbean have made substantial progress in improving access to secondary education, but the quality of education continues to lag behind that of advanced nations and developing country peers in East Asia. What may become more important as new automation technologies are adopted in the region is adult learning and retraining programs. It is possible that transformations in the workplace will happen mid-career for many. Workers will need to adapt and adjust, particularly by changing the set of tasks performed at work. To minimize the adjustment costs borne by workers, governments should have programs that help workers upskill and retrain.

Rethinking labor regulations and social protection policies

Last but not least, the accelerated transformation of jobs calls for a rethinking of labor regulations and social protection policies. Countries in Latin America and the Caribbean developed an institutional architecture geared to wage earners working in the formal sector. Much of the regulation focused on employer-employee relationships, while social protection programs were job-based. This architecture led to rigidity and exclusion in an environment where many workers were self-employed or operated at the margins of formality.

Premature deindustrialization, the increasing servicification of the economy, and the growing reliance on electronic platforms raise doubts that wage employment will increase substantially in the coming years. At the same time, new technologies make activities and earnings much more visible to the authorities. For example, social security contributions based on earnings processed through electronic platforms are becoming increasingly possible. The last pillar of the policy agenda implied by this report thus concerns the flexible regulation of the emerging forms of work in a way that encourages employment and supports formalization, thereby expanding the coverage of social protection to larger segments of the population.

Notes

1. See Herrendorf, Rogerson, and Valentinyi (2013) for a comprehensive review of the literature.
2. This is known in the literature as Baumol's disease.
3. The countries for which available comparable data exist for the analysis are Argentina, Bolivia, Brazil, Chile, Colombia, Costa Rica, Mexico, Peru, and República Bolivariana de Venezuela.

References

Ghani, E., and H. Kharas. 2010. "The Service Revolution." Brief 54595, World Bank, Washington, DC.

Herrendorf, B., Rogerson, R., and A. Valentinyi. 2013. "Two Perspectives on Preferences and Structural Transformation." *American Economic Review* 103 (7): 2752–89.

Rodrik, Dani. 2016. "Premature Deindustrialization." *Journal of Economic Growth* 21 (1): 1–33.

World Bank. 2019. *World Development Report 2019: The Changing Nature of Work.* Washington, DC: World Bank.

What is structural transformation? | 1

Structural transformation, a distinctive feature of economic growth, occurs when a sustained period of rising income and living standards coincides with changes in the distribution of economic activity across three broad sectors of an economy—agriculture, industry, and services.[1] Structural transformation is of interest to analysts because of its intimate ties to trends in productivity, regional income convergence, labor force participation, urbanization, business cycles, wage inequality, and many other facets of development. These ties often open avenues for policy interventions contending that the existing allocation of activity across sectors is inefficient.

Economic activity at the sectoral level is generally measured through employment shares, value-added shares, and final consumption expenditure shares. Although these measures are related and broadly display the same patterns, they are in fact distinct. Both employment and value-added shares refer to production side measures, whereas final consumption expenditure shares refers to the consumption side. Box 1.1 highlights the main issues associated with the different measures of sectoral economic activity. Because of data availability and a focus on

productivity, this report concentrates on the production side measures.

The sizable literature documenting the patterns of structural transformation in developed countries has established three stylized facts. First, at lower income levels agriculture accounts for a dominant share of resources and output. Second, as an economy grows, the agriculture sector shrinks in terms of both employment and value-added share (figure 1.1, panel a), while the other two sectors, industrial and services, increase in prominence (figure 1.1, panels b and c). Initially, both the industrial and services sectors expand. However, unlike services, which continue to grow at higher levels of income, the industrial sector eventually reaches a peak and then begins contracting (see figure 1.1, panels b and c).[2] This pattern is commonly known as the "hump shape" of industry.[3] More recent evidence uncovered by Buera and Kaboski (2012a, 2012b) suggests that growth in services value added accelerates at around $8,100 (1990 international dollars). Moreover, this acceleration coincides with a decrease in the nominal value-added share for the industrial sector.

Although the lack of long time series data has limited analysis of the structural transformation of developing countries, there is

BOX 1.1   **Measuring structural transformation**

Structural transformation involves changes through time in the amount of economic activity occurring in sectors. But what is the best way to measure economic activity? And does it matter which units are used?

Three measures are conventionally used to measure economic activity at the sectoral level: employment shares, value-added shares, and final consumption expenditure shares. Two of these measures—employment shares and value-added shares—are measures of production, whereas final consumption expenditure shares are a measure of consumption. Although the three measures are sometimes thought to be interchangeable, some important differences should be noted, particularly for empirical work. As Herrendorf, Rogerson, and Valentinyi (2013) point out, even though the measures often display the same qualitative behavior, the quantitative implications can be very different, and at times even the qualitative behavior can differ.

Perhaps the starkest conceptual distinction between these measures is that of production versus consumption. This distinction can be traced back to the difference between the concepts of value added and final output and how national accounts are constructed. In their example, Herrendorf, Rogerson, and Valentinyi (2013) illustrate clearly the distinction between the measures. The entire cost of a cotton shirt is recorded as a final consumption expenditure of manufacturing because it is a good as opposed to a service. However, the accounting of value-added attributes one component to the agriculture sector (the cotton used in the shirt), another to the industrial sector (the transformation of cotton into a shirt), and yet another to the services sector (the distribution and retail services where the shirt was purchased). It follows that both quantities and prices may differ between the value added and the final expenditure, suggesting there is no reason to expect the implied shares to exhibit similar behavior.

The measures relating to production may also contain different information. For example, in 1966 Kuznets noted that during the early days of the US economy the share of employment in services increased, while the value-added share remained almost constant. More recently, Rodrik (2016, 2) notes that "in the United States manufacturing industries' share of total employment has steadily fallen since the 1950s, coming down from around a quarter of the workforce to less than a tenth today. Meanwhile, manufacturing valued added has remained a constant share of gross domestic product at constant prices—a testament to differentially rapid labor productivity growth in this sector." Both observations point to the different effects that technological progress can have on the different measures of structural transformation. The rise of labor-saving automation technologies may deepen this pattern, further reducing employment shares while maintaining or increasing value-added shares.

Beyond conceptual distinctions, each measure presents some additional limitations. Data availability generally drives researchers to measure employment shares by calculating the number of workers in each sector. However, employment may not reflect changes in true labor input. For example, systematic differences in hours worked or in human capital per worker across sectors vary with the level of development. Finally, as noted by Herrendorf, Rogerson, and Valentinyi (2013, 7) "for the case of value-added and consumption expenditure shares, a key issue arises from the need to distinguish between changes in quantities and prices. This is often difficult empirically because reliable data on relative price comparisons across countries are hard to come by. In addition, consumption and production need not coincide because of the presence of investment and of imports and exports, so that neither measure alone is sufficient."

FIGURE 1.1   Structural transformation by sector, selected LAC countries and rest of world

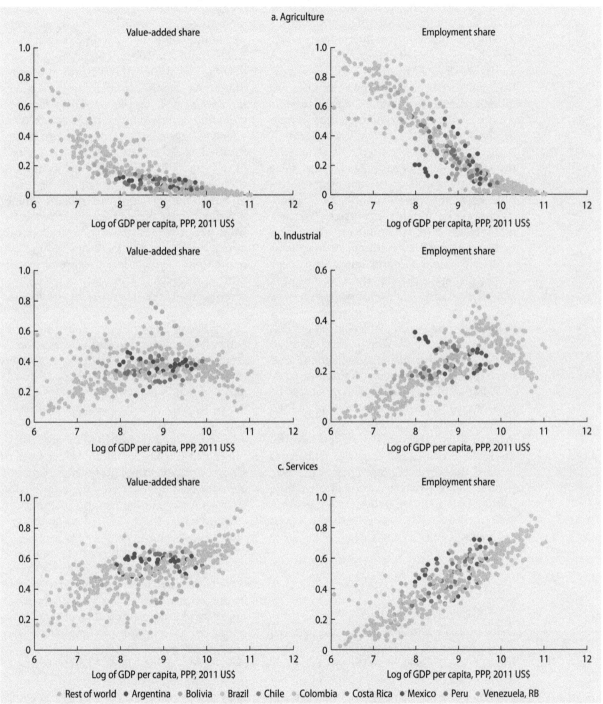

Sources: Original calculations for this publication. Value-added and employment data: Groningen Growth and Development Centre (GGDC), 10-Sector Database (Timmer, de Vries, and de Vries 2015); GDP: Penn World Tables (Feenstra, Inklaar, and Timmer 2015).
Note: The graphs plot the sectoral value-added shares and sectoral employment shares against the log of GDP per capita (in 2011 US dollars, PPP-adjusted). Data are for nine countries (Argentina, Bolivia, Brazil, Chile, Colombia, Costa Rica, Mexico, Peru, and República Bolivariana de Venezuela) in the LAC region and 31 countries in the rest of the world. Data are plotted for every five years from 1961 to 2011. GDP = gross domestic product; LAC = Latin America and the Caribbean; PPP = purchasing power parity.

now substantial evidence that the patterns of structural transformation evident in developed countries broadly hold true for developing countries as well. In poorer countries, larger shares of employment and value added are devoted to the agriculture sector, whereas lower-middle-income countries are industrializing, and higher-middle-income countries are deindustrializing as the growth of their services sector has accelerated. Although the broad patterns of structural transformation in developing economies are consistent with the experience of developed economies, there is substantial heterogeneity among developing countries. Furthermore, recent evidence points to a disruption or stunting of the traditional development ladder because developing countries appear to be starting the deindustrialization process at earlier stages of development—that is, at lower levels of gross domestic product (GDP) per capita—and achieving lower peak industry shares. This phenomenon has been dubbed "premature deindustrialization," and it is explored at length later in this chapter.

What explains these stylized facts of structural transformation? Is this change in the economic structure of countries' growth maximizing or desirable? Many analysts have argued that the transition toward the lower productivity and lower productivity growth services sector is problematic because productivity growth will stall and with it the growth of an economy. The next section turns to these questions.

What drives structural transformation?

Determining whether the observed patterns of transformation are efficient requires understanding what forces drive the process. Over the last two decades, research has taken big steps toward identifying the fundamental mechanisms underlying structural transformation. Although the search for newer explanations continues, two contrasting mechanisms have attracted most of the scrutiny.

The first mechanism postulates that the income elasticity of demand varies across sectoral goods. Put differently, consumers' preferences are nonhomothetic (Kongsamut, Rebelo, and Xie 2001). Thus as an economy becomes wealthier, the sectoral allocation of activity changes in response to changes induced by shifts in the household expenditure, which moves away from agricultural goods as subsistence food requirements are fulfilled. In other words, in the early stages of development households spend most of their budget on food. As countries grow and income per capita increases, households that have already met their needs for food begin to purchase industrial goods and services. At higher levels of income, households devote a larger share of expenditures to services. This mechanism is often referred to in the literature as the income effect.

The second mechanism posits that exogenous technological growth differs across sectors, which generates long-term changes in the relative prices of sectoral goods (Baumol 1967; Ngai and Pissarides 2007). According to this mechanism, economic activity moves away from the agriculture sector because technological growth in the sector outpaces technological growth elsewhere, making agricultural goods cheaper over time. Under the assumption that sectoral goods are complements in consumption, the relative decline in agricultural prices implies a lower allocation of the household budget to agricultural goods. The main implication of this theory is that higher relative productivity growth in one sector pushes workers toward the lower productivity growth sectors (again, under the assumption of complementarity of sectoral goods in consumption and in closed economy models). Therefore, higher growth in the productivity of the industrial sector would tend to push workers toward the services sector. Because of the association with changes in relative prices, this mechanism is known as the price effect.[4]

Structural transformation and the role of trade

Observers from academia and policy institutions argue that a rise in global trade is fostering deindustrialization in many countries. Economies that lack a comparative advantage in industrial production import these goods and therefore allocate productive resources to the other sectors.

Although the bulk of the literature has concentrated on closed economy models, some studies highlight how trade influences the pattern of transformation. A country experiencing an improvement in comparative advantage on the back of relatively high technological growth in one of the sectors will see greater allocation of activity to the sector (Matsuyama 2009). Thus trade opposes the change in allocation induced by the price effects mechanism just outlined. Perhaps the most critical implication of the open economy model is that it allows the behavior of production side measures of transformation—value-added shares and employment—to deviate from the behavior of the consumption expenditure share. This discrepancy in the two types of measures of transformation is observed in the data and is pronounced for some countries.[5]

Few studies have quantitatively appraised the role of trade, and when they have, dissection of the transformation of the Republic of Korea has been at the forefront. Uy, Yi, and Zhang (2013) and Teignier (2018) find the trade-induced mechanism to be critical to understanding the Korean experience. Nevertheless, comparing the labor allocation in Korea to allocations in countries at a similar level of development that industrialized before trade was prevalent does not reveal a remarkable deviation. An analysis of a larger set of countries reveals that, barring some cases, trade has played a secondary role to the main mechanisms just described (Święcki 2017). Trade, however, occupies center stage in smaller economies and accordingly has been crucial in determining their path of structural transformation.

Sinha (2019a) analyzes the relative strength of five different channels—including trading patterns—in accounting for the observed share of industrial employment in economies in the Latin America and the Caribbean (LAC) region. The author finds limited support in favor of the comparative advantage hypothesis. Countries with high industrial shares in employment do not derive a large enough share of the value added from industrial exports relative to countries with a low industrial employment share to justify the glaring industrial share gap between the two groups. According to the analysis, differences in trade shares account for only a tenth of the 11 percentage point gap between the LAC sample and a set of benchmark advanced countries over the 1995–2011 time frame.

Sinha notes, however, that even though little evidence supports the comparative advantage hypothesis, other trade-induced forces may be at play. For example, trade may interact with preferences on the consumption side of the economy as household expenditure shares adjust to trade. For instance, trade may introduce new products and varieties in the domestic market that in turn utilize domestically produced industrial inputs. Thus when consumption shifts toward these new products and varieties, a share of the household expenditure also moves toward domestically produced industrial inputs indirectly. Similarly, sectoral linkages and productivity gaps may also respond to trade shocks.

Structural transformation and the role of intermediate goods

Following the bulk of the literature on structural transformation, this study team adopted the assumption that each economic sector has a production function that takes labor and capital as inputs for production. Recently, studies have begun looking at the relationship between sectoral linkages and structural transformation. Specifically, the new models explicitly account for the fact that the output of one sector is often used as an input for another sector. This section explores the potentially important role of intermediate goods in explaining patterns of structural transformation.

Berlingieri (2013) documents that shifts in input-output relationships could account for roughly a quarter of the decline in the manufacturing employment share in the postwar United States. Using input-output data for the United States for 1947–2002, Berlingieri finds that 50 percent of the employment growth and 94 percent of the GDP growth of the services sector are explained by the growth of service subsectors—professional and business services and finance and real estate—in which final demand plays a relatively small role.[6] He highlights two important channels that help explain the decline of manufacturing and the rise of services in the United States: changes in the composition of intermediates and their sourcing mode. Specifically, he suggests that service activities that were performed within a manufacturing firm are now being outsourced to firms specializing in these services. In this setting, changes in intermediate demand lead to a reallocation of labor across sectors. He concludes that the sole evolution of the input-output structure of the economy accounts for 36 percent of the total increase in service employment and 25 percent of the decline in manufacturing. Sinha (2019a) uses a similar accounting framework and finds that differences in sectoral linkages could account for a third of the gap in the industrial share of employment across the LAC region and advanced comparator economies over 1995–2011.

In a background paper for this report, Sinha (2019b) analyzes the sectoral allocation of labor in eight Latin American economies with an emphasis on whether changes in distortions in intermediate markets can have a quantitatively meaningful impact on the industrial share of employment. In line with the structural transformation literature, the main thrust of his model is that economic sectors experience different rates of exogenous productivity growth. This sector-biased productivity growth leads in turn to changes in the relative prices of sectoral outputs. The pivotal extension of the model is that it allows for price effects on the production side as well by allowing for a nonunitary elasticity of substitution across intermediates from different sectors. Thus sector-biased productivity growth affects changes in intermediate expenditures and changes in final consumption expenditures.

Sinha (2019b) also documents that, as in the United States, in Latin American economies shifts in intermediate expenditure shares are significant and often larger in magnitude compared with the shifts in final consumption shares. Two important results from this exercise are worth highlighting. First, changes in distortions create a contractionary pressure on the industrial employment in five countries in the sample. Second, distortions in the use of service inputs relative to industrial inputs explain 80–90 percent of the counterfactual change. When service input distortions are held at their historical minimum (over the 1995–2011 time frame of the analysis), the industrial sector gains a share of 2.5 percentage points on average because sectoral inputs are estimated to be complements in the production function. Thus reducing distortion in the intermediate service market makes the inputs relatively cheaper, and so all sectors will tend to increase the share of nonservice inputs. In summary, the analysis establishes that distortions play a quantitatively significant role in intermediate markets in determining the sectoral allocation of labor in the LAC region.

The LAC experience

Although the stylized facts of structural transformation are robust across countries, the patterns of transformation are far from identical. The cross-country variations vary systematically across certain dimensions, which supports the argument that the sectoral allocation may not be efficient in some instances. This section turns to the experience of the LAC economies and how they compare with the path observed for today's developed countries and for their developing economy peers.

Since the seminal paper by Rodrik (2016), much attention has been devoted to the notion of the premature deindustrialization of developing countries, particularly Latin American economies. The concept of deindustrialization is not new. Advanced economies have been deindustrializing for decades and have shifted into a postindustrial phase of development. However, Rodrik (2016, 2) documents a "less noticed trend over the last three decades which is even more striking, and puzzling, a pattern of de-industrialization in low- and middle-income countries. . . . The hump-shaped relationship between industrialization (measured by employment or output shares) and incomes has shifted downwards and moved closer to the origin." In other words, the industrial share at its peak in these countries is lower than the ones achieved in the past by developed countries, and the peak materializes at lower levels of income per capita. The study team replicated the analysis

for the manufacturing sector and can confirm both visually and statistically that the path for LAC countries differs from that of today's developed nations. As stated earlier, LAC economies have entered the deindustrialization phase earlier in the development process (lower GDP per capita) and have achieved lower peaks (see figure 1.2).[7]

Although a broad pattern of premature deindustrialization is true for LAC countries, there is heterogeneity among them. Consistent with their level of development, LAC economies are at different stages of deindustrialization (see figure 1.3, panel a, for real value-added shares and panel b for employment shares). At one end are countries such as Argentina and Chile with the highest development levels and a clear downward trend in the share of employment in industry. At the other end, Bolivia, with the lowest level of development in the sample, is still industrializing—that is, the share of employment

FIGURE 1.2   Patterns of industrialization across LAC and high-income countries

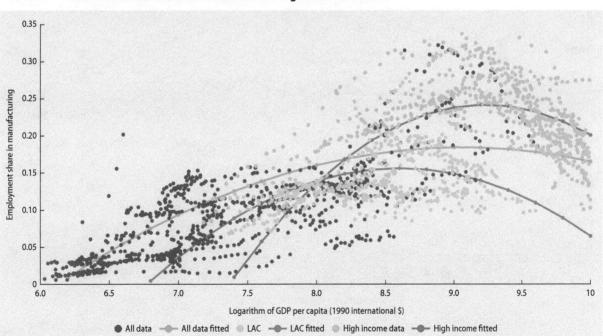

Sources: Original calculations for this publication using Groningen Growth and Development Centre (GGDC)'s 10-Sector Database (Timmer, de Vries, and de Vries 2015); Maddison Database (Bolt et al. 2018).
Note: Graph depicts the share of manufacturing on the logarithm of GDP per capita (expressed in 1990 international dollars). Solid lines are simulated shares from a quadratic fit. Data cover the period 1950–2012 for 40 countries. Graph is based on the World Bank's 2012 classification of countries by income. GDP = gross domestic product; LAC = Latin America and the Caribbean.

FIGURE 1.3   **Value-added and employment shares by sector: Selected LAC countries, 1950–2010**

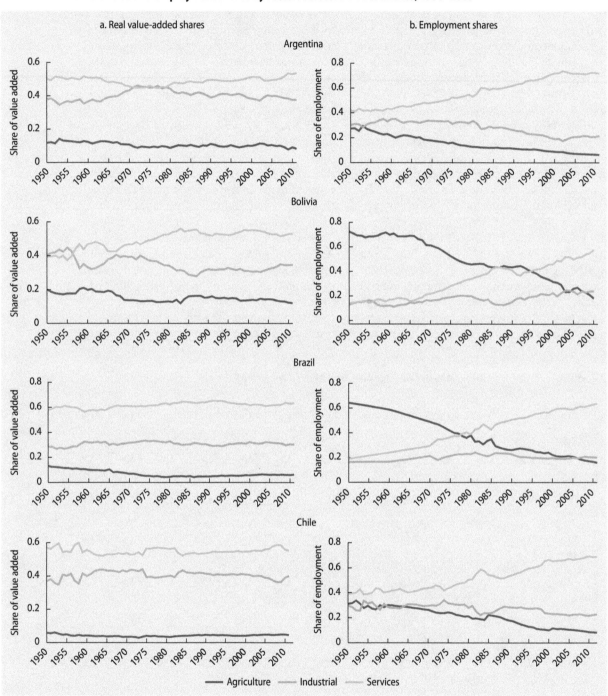

figure continues next page

FIGURE 1.3   **Value-added and employment shares by sector: Selected LAC countries, 1950–2010** *(Continued)*

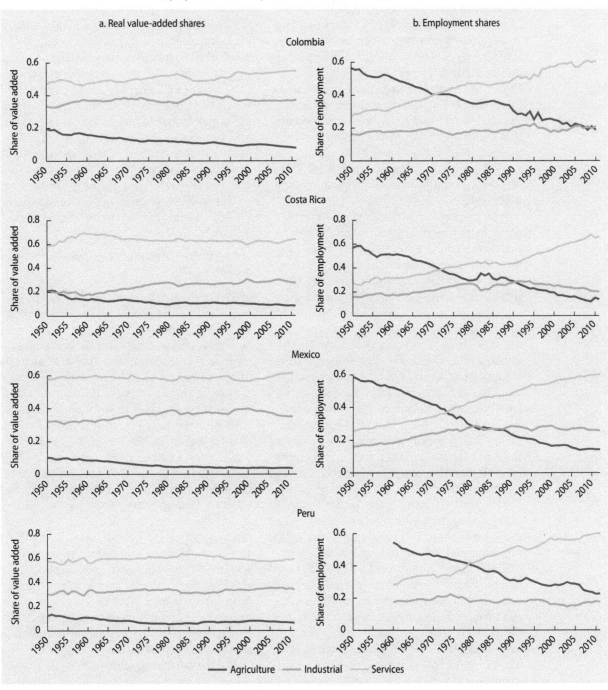

a. Real value-added shares

b. Employment shares

Agriculture   Industrial   Services

Sources: Original calculations for this publication. Employment and value-added data: Groningen Growth and Development Centre (GGDC), 10-Sector Database (Timmer, de Vries, and de Vries 2015); GDP: Penn World Tables (Feenstra, Inklaar, and Timmer 2015).
Note: All value-added values are computed at 2005 local currency units. GDP = gross domestic product; LAC = Latin America and the Caribbean.

in industry is actually growing. Somewhere in between are countries such as Brazil and Mexico, which display small declines and stable shares of employment in industry, respectively. To be clear, this finding does not imply that premature deindustrialization is not occurring or is more muted than expected. Given their development levels, Brazil and Mexico have industrial sectors that are smaller than what developed economies achieved at Brazil and Mexico's income level. Moreover, countries such as Bolivia and Peru should be industrializing at a much higher pace.

The changes in employment shares are much more pronounced than the changes in real value-added shares. This is consistent with the experience of the United States, where the employment share drop has been significantly more pronounced than the drop in real value added. This evidence points to the rapid growth of labor productivity in the industrial sector. As noted by Rodrik (2016, 2), "in the United States manufacturing industries' share of total employment has steadily fallen since the 1950s, coming down from around a quarter of the workforce to less than a tenth today. Meanwhile, manufacturing valued added has remained a constant share of GDP at constant prices—a testament to differentially rapid labor productivity growth in this sector."

One final clarifying point is that analysis of structural transformation and deindustrialization is based on comparing the relative importance of sectors and not absolute levels of employment or value added. In fact, the number of employed people in the industrial sector has grown over time in almost all LAC countries, including Argentina and Chile (see figure 1.4), where deindustrialization has been under way for decades. However, the number of people employed in the services sector has skyrocketed—even in less developed economies such as Bolivia—leading to a falling relative share of employment in industry.

Therefore, the story of deindustrialization in the LAC region is not one of shuttered factories and mass layoffs of factory workers. Instead, it is a story of a stunted industrialization process whereby the industrial sector was unable to grow and create jobs over time as it did in developed economies. In part, this story may be related to the history behind the industrialization phase in LAC countries. Economies began the industrialization process under the banner of the old school industrial policies of protectionism and subsidies. As globalization evolved, the industrial sector of LAC countries largely did not successfully integrate into global value chains. The industrial sector was therefore unable to grow, limited by the size of domestic and, in some cases, regional markets.

Is premature deindustrialization a problem?

Since the work of Rodrik (2016), scholars and policy makers have become concerned about the onset of premature deindustrialization in countries undergoing their earlier stages of structural transformation. The reallocation of resources out of industry into services is starting at lower levels of development and at lower peaks than in developed nations. This property of structural transformation is interpreted as reflecting an inefficient reallocation of labor due to some underlying distortions—that is, Latin America should be deindustrializing at a slower pace (and, for the least developed countries, industrializing at a faster pace). However, there is no theoretically grounded benchmark of efficiency against which to compare the data that justifies the conclusion of inefficiency. Could it be that resources are flowing out of industry sooner than in other countries because the underlying drivers of structural change are efficiently calling for such a pattern of deindustrialization?

On the one hand, scholars such as Rodrik (2016) posit that the decline in industry shares is not good news for developing countries because it blocks the main avenue for economic convergence. This assertion is rooted in the fact that manufacturing (the main component of the industrial sector) not only has higher productivity, but also higher

FIGURE 1.4   Absolute total level of employment by sector: Selected LAC countries, 1950–2010

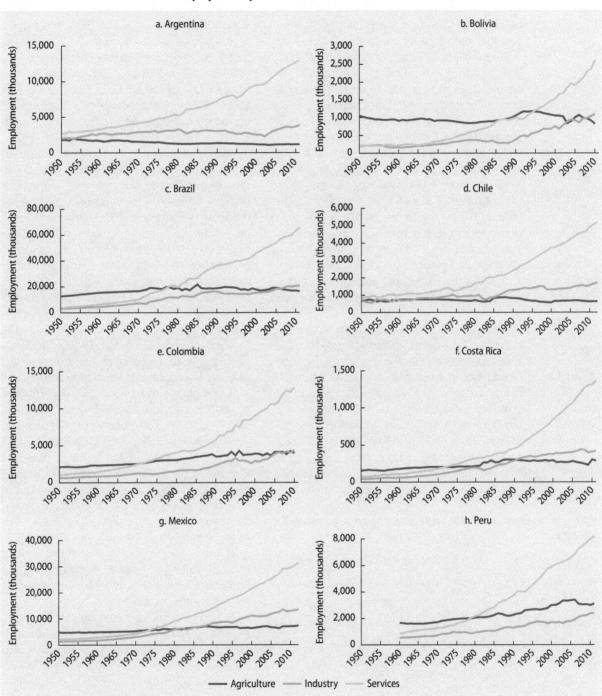

Source: Original calculations for this publication using the Groningen Growth and Development Centre (GGDC)'s 10-Sector Database (Timmer, de Vries, and de Vries 2015).
Note: LAC = Latin America and the Caribbean.

productivity growth. Indeed, there is evidence that manufacturing plays a critical role in the catch-up process because it exhibits unconditional convergence in labor productivity unlike other sectors of the economy (Rodrik 2012). Moreover, there is general skepticism that services can serve as an alternative engine for growth. Although high-productivity and tradable services are available such as information and communications technology (ICT) and finance, they are generally highly skill-intensive and cannot absorb large numbers of unskilled workers in the way that manufacturing does (or at least did in the past). Other service subsectors tend to be less dynamic (lower productivity growth) or nontradable, which limits their ability to be an engine of growth because they are constrained by the size of the domestic market.

On the other hand, the deindustrialization patterns observed in LAC countries may be the result of changes in the underlying drivers of structural transformation and thus the efficient (growth-maximizing) path. In other words, efforts to stop or reverse deindustrialization patterns would create distortions in the economy that ultimately would result in lower overall growth. In a background paper for this report, Fattal Jaef (2019) evaluates the patterns of structural change in the LAC region through the lens of a standard three-sector

general equilibrium model with income and relative price effects in consumption. The author derives from this model a benchmark of efficiency against which to characterize the pattern of deindustrialization in the data.

Using this model of structural transformation, Fattal Jaef identifies the efficient baseline by identifying the paths of labor allocation across sectors implied by the model after feeding it estimated paths of sectoral labor productivities and the observed growth in real expenditure per capita. The author then evaluates the inefficiency of the observed premature deindustrialization hypothesis by comparing the labor allocations in the data against the model. In this context, it is possible to characterize a pattern of deindustrialization as premature and inefficient if the decline of employment of manufacturing occurs at a rate faster than the one predicted by the benchmark model. For some countries, manufacturing activity is still on the rise. In this case, the industrialization is labeled sluggish if manufacturing employment in the data increases at a slower pace than is predicted by the model.

The theory, definitions, and estimates of sectoral productivity growth, and the observed path of aggregate real expenditure per capita, give rise to evidence of premature deindustrialization in Latin America starting in the 1980s (see figure 1.5). For the period 1950–1980, the benchmark model of structural change tracks the observed manufacturing employment share very closely. For 1980 onward, however, the model predicts that manufacturing employment should have continued to expand. Instead, the data indicate a reversal of the trend as employment began to decline.

Figure 1.5 shows that, as suggested by Rodrik (2016), there is evidence of premature deindustrialization occurring in Latin America as of the mid-1970s, years in which the model continues to exhibit a rising share of manufacturing employment, whereas the share begins to decline in the data.

To make sense of the model's predicted dynamics, figure 1.6 illustrates the estimated paths of relative prices and real consumption per capita for Latin America (average).

FIGURE 1.5   **Premature deindustrialization: LAC region (average), 1950–2010**

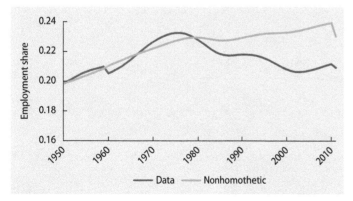

Source: Fattal Jaef 2019.
Note: Figure shows average employment shares in industry. The nonhomothetic line refers to model fit. LAC = Latin America and the Caribbean.

FIGURE 1.6 **Relative prices and real consumption per capita: LAC region (average), 1950–2010**

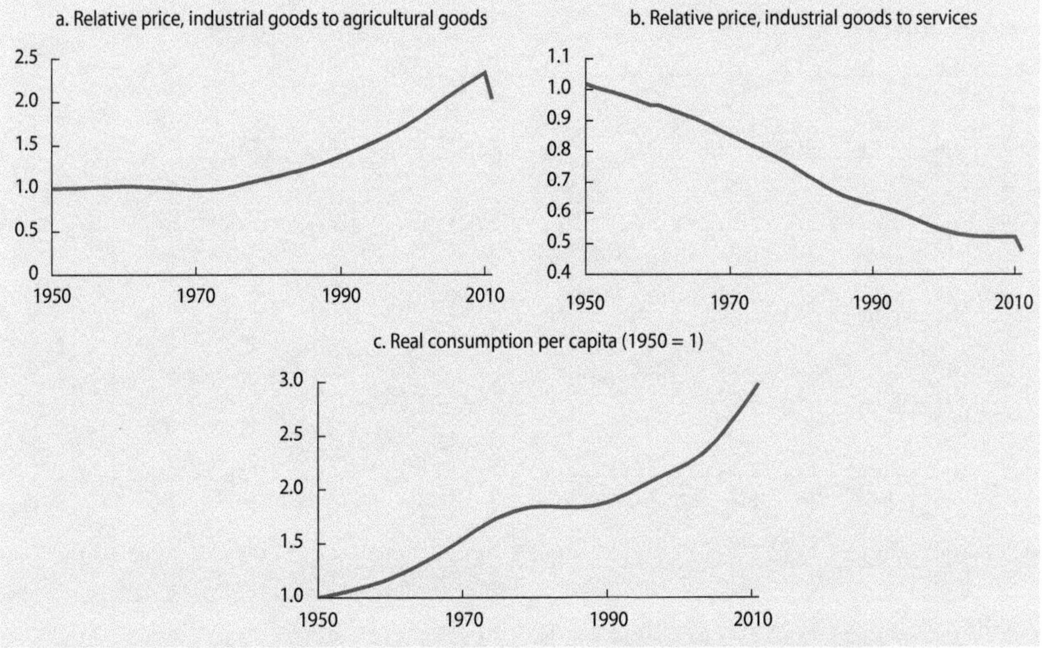

a. Relative price, industrial goods to agricultural goods

b. Relative price, industrial goods to services

c. Real consumption per capita (1950 = 1)

Sources: Original calculations for this publication using the Groningen Growth and Development Centre (GGDC)'s 10-Sector Database (Timmer, de Vries, and de Vries 2015); Penn World Tables (Feenstra, Inklaar, and Timmer 2015).
Note: LAC = Latin America and the Caribbean.

The relative price of industrial to agricultural goods remains stagnant between 1950 and 1970, rising notably thereafter (panel a). At the same time, industrial goods cheapen relative to services throughout the entire period, albeit with a slowdown in the mid-2000s (panel b). Finally, real consumption grows steadily until the 1980s, remaining stagnant until the end of that decade after which it resumes its growth trajectory (panel c).

In the benchmark model, the low-income elasticity of agricultural goods (relative to industrial goods) induces a reallocation from agriculture to the industrial sector. Quantitatively, it follows that the relative strengths of these channels make the model and the data remarkably close, at least until the 1980s. Thereafter, because relative price trends do not change and real consumption continues to grow, the model predicts that the region should have continued to industrialize. The data, however, show a significant decline. It is this divergence between data and the benchmark model

that here is called premature deindustrialization—specifically, in the sense that it implies an inefficiency.

Investigation of each of the seven countries in the sample reveals substantial heterogeneity in the patterns of structural change, with manufacturing activity still rising in some countries (see figure 1.7). Argentina is perhaps the most salient case of premature deindustrialization, followed by Chile and Peru. The model seems to follow the data closely for Colombia and Brazil, whereas Mexico is an outlier in the sense that its observed industrialization is higher than the benchmark prediction in contrast with the pattern of the average.

In addition to assessing the degree of premature deindustrialization, Fattal Jaef (2019) offers a quantitative assessment of the aggregate output costs associated with this process. He finds that premature deindustrialization is not very costly to the LAC region in terms of output and aggregate productivity. For the region as a whole, the output

FIGURE 1.7 **Labor allocation in manufacturing: Selected LAC countries, 1950–2010**

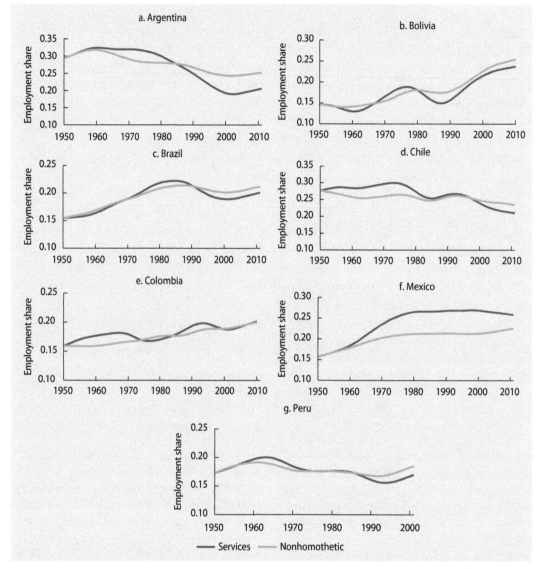

Source: Fattal Jaef 2019.
Note: LAC = Latin America and the Caribbean.

costs are on the order of 0.1 percent—that is, aggregate output would be 0.1 percent higher if the region had followed the path predicted by the model. Obviously, the cost estimates are highly dependent on the choice of the efficient benchmark. Thus the results should be interpreted with caution.

At first sight, under the given trade-offs of the underlying model, one interpretation of these findings is that the costs of premature

deindustrialization do not give policy makers enough incentive to justify implementation of industrial policies aimed at remedying it. Taking into account how difficult it is to identify the policy that will undo the ongoing distortion, together with the stickiness of the subsidies and benefits put in place to incentivize manufacturing activity, the available gains do not seem to justify the costs. Alternatively, these findings could be interpreted as strengthening the case for improving fundamentals rather than seeking to change the course of structural change through policy instruments. One improvement that would bring about a slowdown of deindustrialization, or a strengthening of ongoing industrialization, is increasing the productivity of the services sector.

A second interpretation of the findings is that the model leaves out many features of the manufacturing sector that make it desirable to subsidize its operations. Thus the output cost calculations are just the lower bounds of the full costs of premature deindustrialization. Rodrik (2016) outlines various reasons why manufacturing is special relative to other sectors of an economy—features that have not been explicitly captured in the model. One of these features that would have first-order welfare effects is the prominent role typically played by manufacturing in absorbing low-skilled workers. A premature bypassing of industrial activity would reduce the demand for low-skilled workers, bringing with it an increase in the skill premium and therefore an increase in inequality.

All this being said, the findings suggest that expensive industrial policies that introduce more distortions in the economy are not readily warranted. Because of the complexities of implementing such policies, their stickiness, and the discretion underlying the choice of winners and losers, confronting these risks may not be worthwhile. This is not to say that there is no space for government policy to address latent issues in the industrial sector. In fact, as developed further in chapter 2, labor productivity in the LAC industrial sector significantly lags that of the United States. In particular, it appears there are significant distortions in the sector that would result in a firm size distribution heavily skewed toward small and microenterprises. In addition, as new technologies are incorporated into the production processes, complementary investments in human capital and infrastructure, as well as modernization of regulatory frameworks, will be central to the ongoing competitiveness of the industrial sector.

Conclusions

Evidence suggests that trade has not been a major factor in explaining the observed patterns of the changing economic structure of the LAC region. Although trade is important in some specific cases, such as Korea and some smaller countries, little evidence points to the comparative advantage hypothesis in explaining the structural change patterns in the LAC region.

The role of intermediate inputs and the input-output relationships between sectors appears to have some quantitative importance in explaining the observed economic structure in LAC and other developing countries. Input-output relationships seem to vary systematically according to the degree of development, with more advanced nations having more interconnected sectors. In a background paper for this report, Sinha (2019b) finds that distortions in intermediate markets may play a quantitatively important role in explaining the size of the industrial sector. Distortions in the sourcing of intermediate service inputs may have a particularly important role. Keeping intermediate service input distortions at their observed minimum over the 1995–2011 period would imply a larger industrial sector by 2–2.5 percentage points—a large effect considering the actual industrial share of about 20 percentage points.

The process of structural transformation documented in detail for a sample of LAC economies for which internationally comparable data exist confirms the findings of Rodrik (2016). The process known as deindustrialization has in fact begun at lower levels of GDP per capita (relative to the experience of advanced nations) and the share of manufacturing in total value added has peaked at lower levels than for advanced nations.

Some additional features of this process are important for the policy debate. First, the deindustrialization process is reflected more acutely in terms of the share of employment rather than the share of value added. This pattern is similar to that observed for the United

States and may be related to the introduction of labor-saving technologies that increase productivity (and help sustain the share of value added) but do not foster job creation.

Second, consistent with the differences among countries in development level, there is substantial heterogeneity in where they stand in the deindustrialization process. For the more developed economies in the LAC region such as Argentina and Chile, the deindustrialization process is marked and has been ongoing for decades. Less developed countries such as Brazil, Colombia, and Mexico exhibit stagnant or slight increases in their share of industrial employment. At the other end, the least developed economy in the study sample, Bolivia, is still industrializing, with a growing share of industrial employment. This finding does not imply that deindustrialization is not occurring in these countries. And yet relative to the performance of advanced nations and given their level of development, these countries should be industrializing at a much faster pace.

Third, an analysis based on shares may present a distorted view of reality. The absolute number of jobs in the industrial sector is steady or increasing in most countries in the region, including in Argentina and Chile, which have been deindustrializing for decades. At the same time, the number of jobs in the services sector has skyrocketed, leading to a declining share of industrial jobs.

Is the deindustrialization process in the LAC region "premature" in the sense of being inefficient? Empirically, it is clear that peak manufacturing shares achieved in LAC economies were lower relative to those achieved by high-income countries, and that the declining shares of industry are happening at lower levels of GDP per capita. Missing from this empirical assessment, however, is an evaluation of whether this was an efficient (growth maximizing) process or the result of inefficiencies or distortions in the economy. A background paper prepared for this report by Fattal Jaef (2019) asserts that, although on average the LAC region has prematurely and inefficiently deindustrialized, the actual output costs associated with this process were relatively small (on the order of 0.1 percent of output).

Thus the premature deindustrialization process observed in the LAC region since the 1980s has not been very costly in terms of output loss. But this is not to say that there is no room for improvement or that there is no scope for government policies to improve the allocation of resources across the economy. The focus should be on raising productivity in all sectors and facilitating the transition of workers and resources among sectors. Indeed, as shown in the next chapter, there are productivity issues in all sectors of the economy. Special attention should be paid, however, to understanding the specific productivity issues in the services sector. Not only is this sector already the main employer in LAC economies, the expectation is that it will continue to grow as countries continue to develop. Moreover, the dearth of data specific to the services sector is particularly worrisome, as there is little evidence on the issues that affect firms in that sector.

Notes

1. *Agriculture* refers to agriculture, forestry, and fishing. Industry refers to mining and quarrying, utilities, construction, and manufacturing. For most countries, manufacturing is the largest component of the industrial sector. Services are all other industries.
2. This phase of development is known as deindustrialization.
3. Studies in the 1950s and 1960s such as those by Chenery (1960), Clark (1951), and Kuznets (1966) contributed to documenting these stylized facts of the structural transformation process. More recently, Herrendorf, Rogerson, and Valentinyi (2014), using data from multiple sources, presented a detailed account of the process covering many countries across the global income distribution. They also provided a comprehensive survey of both the theoretical and the empirical literature.
4. Sector-biased technological change is not a condition needed for relative prices to change. Relative prices can also change if instead sectors differ in how intensively they use certain inputs over others and if the relative supply of these

inputs changes over time. Caselli and Coleman (2001) have explored the shift in the relative abundance of low- and high-skilled labor, and Acemoglu and Guerrieri (2008) have studied the trend in the relative availability of capital and labor during the transformation process.

5. Researchers have also explored the influence of other factors such as the costs associated with the movement of goods (see Adamopoulos 2011; Gollin and Rogerson 2014) and labor (see Dekle and Vandenbroucke 2012; Lee and Wolpin 2006) across sectors. A recent but growing literature is exploring how sectoral linkages interact with the transformation process (Berlingieri 2013; Sposi 2019).

6. In 2002 roughly 83 percent of the output of professional and business services was sold to firms as intermediate inputs, compared with 44 percent for the economy as a whole.

7. With the possible exception of Argentina. It achieved a peak of about 27 percent in manufacturing, which is comparable to that achieved by today's high-income countries.

References

Acemoglu, D., and V. Guerrieri. 2008. "Capital Deepening and Nonbalanced Economic Growth." *Journal of Political Economy* 116 (3): 467–98.

Adamopoulos, T. 2011. "Transportation Costs, Agricultural Productivity, and Cross-Country Income Differences." *International Economic Review* 52 (2): 489–521.

Baumol, W. J. 1967. "Macroeconomics of Unbalanced Growth: The Anatomy of Urban Crisis." *American Economic Review* 57 (3): 415–26.

Berlingieri, G. 2013. "Outsourcing and the Rise in Services." CEP Discussion Paper 1199, Centre for Economic Performance, London School of Economics.

Bolt, J., R. Inklaar, H. de Jong, and J. Luiten van Zanden. 2018. "Rebasing 'Maddison': New Income Comparisons and the Shape of Long-run Economic Development." Maddison Project Working Paper 10, Groningen Growth and Development Centre (GGDC), Groningen, The Netherlands.

Buera, F. J., and J. P. Kaboski. 2012a. "The Rise of the Service Economy." *American Economic Review* 102 (6): 2540–69.

Buera, F. J., and J. P. Kaboski. 2012b. "Scale and the Origins of Structural Change." *Journal of Economic Theory* 147 (2): 684–712.

Caselli, F., and W. J. Coleman II. 2001. "The US Structural Transformation and Regional Convergence: A Reinterpretation." *Journal of Political Economy* 109 (3): 584–616.

Chenery, H. B. 1960. "Patterns of Industrial Growth." *American Economic Review* 50 (4): 624–54.

Clark, C. 1951. *The Conditions of Economic Progress*. London: Macmillan.

Dekle, R., and G. Vandenbroucke. 2012. "A Quantitative Analysis of China's Structural Transformation." *Journal of Economic Dynamics and Control* 36 (1): 119–35.

Fattal Jaef, R. N. 2019. "A Quantitative Evaluation of the Premature Deindustrialization Hypothesis in Latin America." Working paper, World Bank, Washington, DC.

Feenstra, R. C., R. Inklaar, and M. P. Timmer. 2015. "The Next Generation of the Penn World Table." *American Economic Review* 105 (10): 3150–82. Available for download at www.ggdc.net/pwt.

Gollin, D., and R. Rogerson. 2014. "Productivity, Transport Costs and Subsistence Agriculture." *Journal of Development Economics* 107: 38–48.

Herrendorf, B., R. Rogerson, and A. Valentinyi. 2013. "Two Perspectives on Preferences and Structural Transformation." *American Economic Review* 103 (7): 2752–89.

Herrendorf, B., R. Rogerson, and A. Valentinyi. 2014. "Growth and Structural Transformation." In *Handbook of Economic Growth*, 2: 855–941. Amsterdam: Elsevier.

Kongsamut, P., S. Rebelo, and D. Xie. 2001. "Beyond Balanced Growth." *Review of Economic Studies* 68 (4): 869–82.

Kuznets, S. 1966. *Modern Economic Growth: Rate, Structure, and Spread*. New Haven, CT: Yale University Press.

Lee, D., and K. I. Wolpin. 2006. "Intersectoral Labor Mobility and the Growth of the Service Sector." *Econometrica* 74 (1): 1–46.

Matsuyama, K. 2009. "Structural Change in an Interdependent World: A Global View of Manufacturing Decline." *Journal of the European Economic Association* 7 (2–3): 478–86.

Ngai, L. R., and C. A. Pissarides. 2007. "Structural Change in a Multisector Model of Growth." *American Economic Review* 97 (1): 429–43.

Rodrik, D. 2012. "Unconditional Convergence in Manufacturing." *Quarterly Journal of Economics* 128 (1): 165–204.

Rodrik, D. 2016. "Premature Deindustrialization." *Journal of Economic Growth* 21 (1): 1–33.

Sinha, R. 2019a. "Distortions in Intermediate Markets and Structural Transformation in Latin America." Working paper, World Bank, Washington, DC.

Sinha, R. 2019b. "What Explains Latin America's Low Share of Industrial Employment?" Policy Research Working Paper 8791, World Bank, Washington, DC.

Sposi, M. J. 2019. "Evolving Comparative Advantage, Sectoral Linkages, and Structural Change." *Journal of Monetary Economics* 103 (May): 75–87.

Święcki, T. 2017. "Intersectoral Distortions and the Welfare Gains from Trade." *Journal of International Economics* 104: 138–56.

Teignier, M. 2018. "The Role of Trade in Structural Transformation." *Journal of Development Economics* 130: 45–65.

Timmer, M. P., G. J. de Vries, and K. de Vries. 2015. "Patterns of Structural Change in Developing Countries." In *Routledge Handbook of Industry and Development,* edited by J. Weiss and M. Tribe, 65–83. Abdingdon-on-Thames, UK: Routledge.

Uy, T., K.-M. Yi, and J. Zhang. 2013. "Structural Change in an Open Economy." *Journal of Monetary Economics* 60 (6): 667–82.

Productivity in the LAC region: A sectoral view

2

Chapter 1 described the phenomenon known as premature deindustrialization and its impact on aggregate productivity growth in economies in the Latin America and the Caribbean (LAC) region. This chapter analyzes the productivity dynamics in each sector and its implications for the future economic structure in the region.

Unfortunately, the picture of productivity in the region is worrisome. Pervasive productivity issues are affecting all sectors of the region's economy (see figure 2.1). On average, the region displays the largest productivity gap (relative to the United States) in the agriculture sector. Even though the gap is smallest in the industrial sector, output per worker represents less than 40 percent of the productivity in the US industrial sector. Perhaps most worrisome is the gap in the services sector because more than 60 percent of the workforce is employed there. The productivity of the services sector in the LAC region is about 25 percent that of the United States.

Although agricultural productivity has increased in the LAC region, it still represents less than 20 percent of the output per worker in the United States. Two main avenues for productivity growth are (1) improving the technical efficiency of producers in view of the existing technology and (2) pushing out the production possibilities frontier by shifting to new, improved technologies. Study of which policies are the most relevant should be conducted at the subnational level. Although soybean production in some areas of Brazil and Argentina appears to be operating at the efficiency frontier, low productivity subsistence farmers can be found in other regions of those countries.

As for the industrial sector—specifically the manufacturing sector—evidence clearly shows a substantial degree of misallocation between firms. The firm-size distribution is skewed toward small and microenterprises. This finding points toward distortions in the market that are preventing the consolidation and growth of the most productive firms. It thus calls for government action instituting policies that foster competition—such as international trade and deepening of regional trade agreements. It also calls for revisions of size-dependent policies (or enforcement) that appear to hamper the growth of productive firms and incentivize informality.

FIGURE 2.1 **Output per worker by sector in LAC region relative to that of United States: Selected countries, 2010**

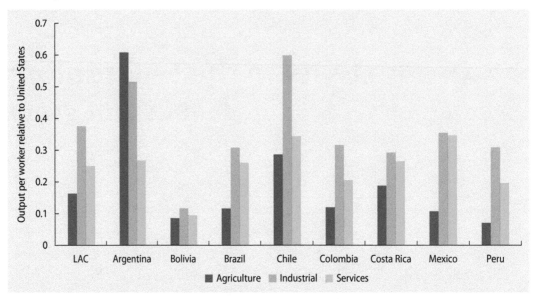

Sources: Original calculations for this publication using Groningen Growth and Development Centre (GGDC)'s 10-Sector Database (Timmer, de Vries, and de Vries 2015); Maddison Database (Bolt et al. 2018).
Note: Graph shows the relative output per worker in eight countries in the LAC region. Sectoral output by country is computed by weighing the total gross domestic product in 2011 international dollars by the share of sectoral value added. LAC = Latin America and the Caribbean.

One of the main messages of this report is that a comprehensive set of policy actions is urgently needed to address productivity issues in the services sector. The sector already employs more than 60 percent of the workforce in the LAC region, and current trends indicate it will continue to grow and be the main source of job creation in the future. Although the scarcity of data on the services sector is an obstacle to a clearer diagnosis, the existing evidence indicates that this sector has a higher degree of misallocation relative to manufacturing.

The shift toward the services sector is not all bad news. This sector is increasingly sharing pro-development characteristics once thought to be the unique domain of manufacturing. The rapid advances in information and communications technology (ICT) have enabled the emergence of service subsectors that are no longer limited by market size because more and more services can be digitally stored, codified, and easily traded (Ghani and Kharas 2010). Meanwhile, the deregulation of services markets has been accompanied by large inflows of foreign direct investment (FDI). Therefore, certain service subsectors are looking more and more like the manufacturing sector (with exposure to trade and inflows of FDI), allowing for greater competition, technology diffusion, and benefits of scale. One caveat is that these services generally require high-skilled workers and so require in turn significant investments in the human capital of the workforce.

Services also provide inputs for the rest of the economy. According to Alvarez et al. (2019), the services sector in the LAC region has the highest degree of forward linkages (also referred to as "push"). In other words, the services sector is heavily intertwined with the rest of the economy and is the most important sector in terms of supplying inputs. The recent trend of "servicification" of manufacturing indicates that more services are being used as inputs in the production of goods (embodied services), and more services are provided to customers bundled in the sale of goods (embedded services). Therefore, the increased productivity of backbone services—such as logistics, ICT, and business services—could ripple throughout the economy, having larger impacts on overall aggregate productivity. In fact, in a background paper for this report, Sinha (2019b) finds that reductions in the cost of service inputs could have quantitatively important effects on the size of the industrial sector.

The structure of the LAC economy is changing and the requirements for productivity growth within sectors are increasing. This chapter turns first to analyzing productivity in the agriculture sector before documenting the productivity dynamics in the industrial and services sectors. It concludes with a discussion of policy interventions to enhance productivity growth in the future.

Productivity in agriculture

What has been the historical performance of growth in agricultural productivity in the LAC region? The question is not an easy one to answer because agricultural productivity and its determinants have often been inaccurately measured and imperfectly understood. Many regions have achieved significant gains in agricultural labor productivity over time, but a large proportion of the gains came from more intensive use of other complementary inputs such as fertilizers, machinery, energy, and irrigation. Because more intensive use of these other inputs raises costs, partial productivity measures such as land and labor productivity are likely to overstate the welfare effects of productivity change. For this reason, a broader concept of agricultural productivity is desirable. The most widely used broader measure is total factor productivity (TFP). TFP is defined as the ratio of aggregate output to aggregate inputs, and so it takes into account all factors involved in the production process (such as land, labor, capital, and other material resources) and compares them with the total crop and livestock output. If total output is

growing more rapidly than total inputs, TFP is said to be increasing. If total output is growing more slowly than total inputs, TFP is said to be decreasing.

Several authors have estimated the long-term average annual growth in agricultural TFP for individual LAC countries or for the region as a whole. Recently, Trindade and Fulginiti (2015) used two different methods—stochastic production frontier and the Malmquist Index—to estimate the growth in agricultural TFP for a subset of Latin American countries over 1969–2009. The results from the two approaches were similar, showing TFP growth averaging about 2.3 percent a year during the first decade of the 21st century. Common among these more recent studies and those that preceded them is a finding of positive average annual growth in agricultural TFP in the LAC region.

Historically, TFP growth has been a major driver of output growth. Figure 2.2 reveals that, beginning in the late 1980s and continuing for more than two decades, TFP growth rose steadily in the LAC region before peaking in 2005. Throughout this period, output growth moved mostly in tandem. After 2005, however, TFP growth dropped sharply, accompanied by a slowdown in output growth. However, output growth did not decelerate as sharply as TFP growth because producers compensated for slowing TFP growth by resorting to input intensification, especially land expansion (see Fuglie et al. 2012).

As expected based on the relationship shown in figure 2.2, when TFP growth is plotted against output growth for individual countries, a strong positive correlation emerges. This relationship holds up not only for countries with modernized, technologically advanced agriculture sectors, but also for countries with large numbers of subsistence-oriented producers (see figure 2.3). In major agricultural producers such as Brazil, Chile, Mexico, and Peru, high TFP growth correlates strongly with high output growth, but the same is true in less developed countries such as Guatemala, Haiti, Honduras, and

FIGURE 2.2   **Agricultural output and TFP growth: LAC region, 1981–2014**

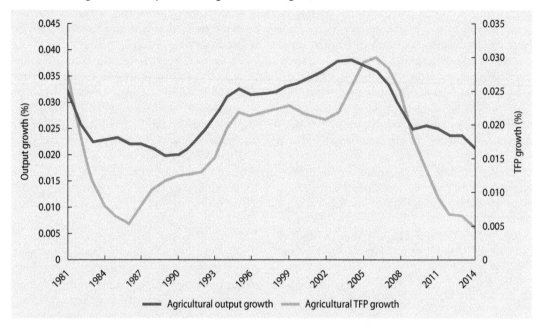

Source: Original calculations for this publication using US Department of Agriculture's agricultural TFP growth indexes database (Fuglie 2015; Fuglie et al. 2012), smoothed using Hodrick-Prescott filter lambda = 6. LAC = Latin America and the Caribbean; TFP = total factor productivity.

FIGURE 2.3   **Correlation between output growth and TFP growth: LAC countries, 2001–14**

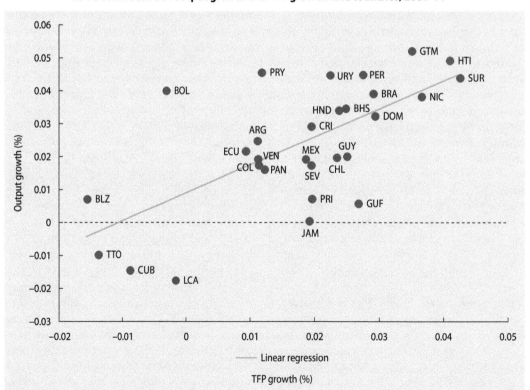

Source: Original calculations for this publication using US Department of Agriculture's agricultural TFP growth indexes database (Fuglie 2015; Fuglie et al. 2012). *Note:* For country abbreviations, see International Organization for Standardization (ISO), http://www.iso.org/obp/ui/#search. LAC = Latin America and the Caribbean; TFP = total factor productivity.

Nicaragua. The latter countries have large populations still employed in agriculture sectors that are modernizing. The strong positive correlation is absent only in two countries, Bolivia and Belize. Bolivia exhibited very strong average output growth but negative TFP growth, whereas Belize recorded output growth despite registering negative TFP growth.

One drawback of analyzing productivity at the regional level is that the regional data conceal a large amount of variability among countries. This variability can be seen in figure 2.4, which decomposes by subregion the agricultural growth recorded between 2005 and 2014. The slowdown in regional TFP growth after 2005 was driven mainly by slower growth in the Southern Cone and Andean regions; TFP growth remained robust in Central America, the Caribbean region, and the Northeast. Meanwhile, land contributed strongly to overall output growth in the Southern Cone and the Northeast, where the agricultural frontier continued to expand rapidly. By contrast, in Central America and the Caribbean region the land frontier contracted as land was converted from agricultural to nonagricultural uses.

Sources of future agricultural productivity growth in the LAC region

Regardless of whether productivity in the agriculture sector is higher, equal to, or lower than productivity in other sectors, the ability of agriculture to contribute to productivity growth in the overall economy depends on the size of the agriculture sector and the rate of agricultural productivity growth. For that reason, it is important to consider the size of the agriculture sector in LAC countries, as well as potential sources of future agricultural productivity growth.

To what extent have LAC agriculture and food systems contributed to economic growth and diversification? The importance of agriculture in a country's economy is traditionally measured as the direct contribution of primary production activities to overall gross domestic product (GDP).[1] Measured this way, the importance of primary agriculture as a share of the

FIGURE 2.4   Growth decomposition: Latin America by region and United States, 2005–14

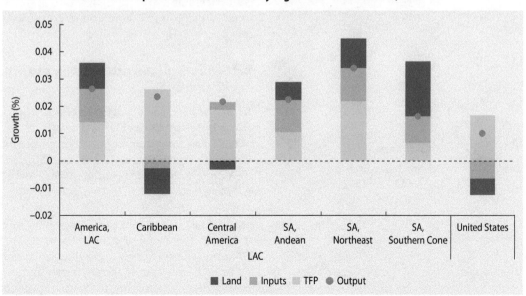

Source: Original calculations for this publication using US Department of Agriculture's TFP growth indexes database (Fuglie 2015; Fuglie et al. 2012).
Note: America, LAC, refers to average of entire region; LAC = Latin America and the Caribbean; SA = South America; TFP = total factor productivity.

FIGURE 2.5   **Relationship between value added and employment in agriculture: Selected LAC countries, 2017**

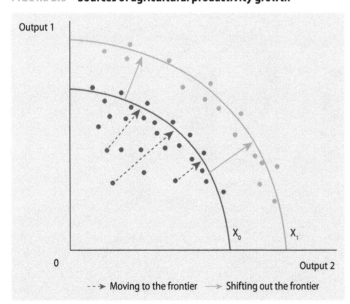

Source: Original calculations for this publication using World Bank's World Development Indicators database, 2019 (https://datacatalog.worldbank.org/dataset/world-development-indicators).
Note: For country abbreviations, see International Organization for Standardization (ISO), http://www.iso.org/obp/ui/#search. GDP = gross domestic product; LAC = Latin America and the Caribbean.

FIGURE 2.6   **Sources of agricultural productivity growth**

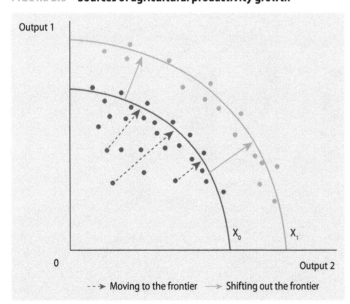

--‣ Moving to the frontier   ⟶ Shifting out the frontier

Source: Original calculations for this publication.

overall economy has declined in many LAC countries, but agriculture and food systems remain a significant contributor to growth (see figure 2.5).

Rate of agricultural productivity growth in LAC countries

As just noted, the ability of agriculture to contribute to productivity growth in the overall economy depends not only on the size of the agriculture sector, but also on the rate of agricultural productivity growth. As shown in figure 2.6. two conceptually distinct sources of growth can be distinguished: (1) that achieved by improving the technical efficiency of producers using the existing technology and (2) that achieved by pushing out the frontier of production possibilities by shifting to new, improved technology.

Moving toward the production possibilities frontier

What scope exists to unlock future productivity growth in agriculture by moving inefficient producers closer to the production possibilities frontier? Recent work carried out in Peru by Espinoza et al. (2018) using a stochastic production metafrontier approach suggests that the potential is likely to vary significantly by region, farmer type, and production system (figure 2.7). In the Costa region, which is dominated by technologically advanced, highly productive commercial agriculture, the vast majority of farmers operate at high levels of efficiency and are clustered close to the efficiency frontier. In the Sierra region, which is dominated by subsistence-oriented smallholder systems characterized by limited use of improved technology and purchased inputs, efficiency levels are more variable and centered farther from the frontier. In the Selva region, which contains a mixture of technologically advanced commercial plantations and technologically lagging subsistence farms, the distribution is very flat and dispersed, indicating the presence of great variability in efficiency levels. These results reveal that in contexts such as the Sierra and Selva regions, considerable scope still exists to accelerate productivity growth by moving inefficient producers closer to the frontier—that is, by giving them the knowledge, resources, and incentives needed to catch up with the most efficient producers.

What are the entry points for helping producers improve their technical efficiency and move closer to the existing production possibilities frontier? A large empirical literature provides insights into factors that can influence technical efficiency at the farm level. Factors that show up consistently as playing a key role are described in the following sections.

Land. In the LAC region as elsewhere, land markets are often imperfect. Transfers of land tend to be subject to cultural, political, or institutional factors that can raise transaction costs and influence outcomes. Ownership of agricultural land is often unequally distributed, and in many countries large numbers of very small farms coexist with small numbers of very large farms. If farm size were unrelated to productivity, it might not matter, but if farm size influences productivity, to the extent that land markets prevent the consolidation or division of agricultural landholdings, productivity could be affected.

What is the relationship between farm size and productivity? Finding the answer to this question has proved to be a perennial puzzle in development economics (Barrett, Bellemare, and Hou 2010; Eastwood, Lipton, and Newell 2010). Building on ideas first articulated by Schumacher (1973) in his classic work *Small Is Beautiful: Economics as If People Mattered*, many empirical

FIGURE 2.7 **Histogram of metatechnical efficiency, Peru, by region**

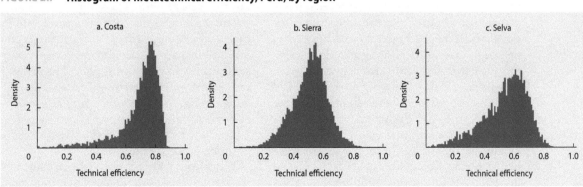

Source: Espinoza et al. 2018.

studies spanning a broad range of contexts have established the stylized fact that farm size and productivity are inversely related. Leading explanations of this phenomenon include imperfections in labor, land, and credit markets (Eswaran and Kotwal 1989; Sen 1966), moral hazard between employers and hired agricultural labor (Feder 1985), aversion to price risk (Barrett 1996), and measurement and identification issues (Assunção and Braido 2007; Benjamin 1992; Carletto, Savastano, and Zezza 2013). However, because the existing theoretical explanations fail to fully explain the observed inverse relationship, the discussion continues over the nature and the strength of the relationship. Indeed, it has influenced the debate over land reform in the LAC region and has highlighted constraints to agricultural productivity in the region, as well as opportunities for unleashing faster productivity growth.

The relationship between farm size and productivity, measured as TFP, may be dynamic, evolving over time and across agricultural regions. Comparing the results of studies of regions within Brazil, Helfand and Taylor (2016) find that in some regions the inverse relationship between farm size and productivity has persisted, whereas in other regions it has become U-shaped. Most interestingly, in a few rapidly modernizing regions a direct positive relationship has begun to replace the inverse relationship. Adding further complexity to the issue, recent work in Mexico suggests that not only could the relationship between farm size and productivity evolve over time, but technological change could occur at differential rates across the farm size spectrum and be accompanied by changes in efficiency levels because producers in different farm size categories vary in their ability to keep up (see box 2.1).

Inputs. Differences between realized output and potential output can result from the failure of producers to use the optimal amount of inputs. To do so, producers must have access to the inputs, as well as the means to acquire them. Both conditions are influenced by farmers' access to input markets, which is highly variable in Latin America and often differs between regions and between farmer typologies within the same country.

Coelli and Rao (2003) estimated the contribution of inputs to TFP growth in agriculture for the period 1980–2003. Using a cross-country approach, they calculated shadow prices and shadow shares of inputs to shed light on factors influencing productivity growth. For land and labor, the shadow shares appear to be meaningful and consistent with the expected factor endowments of the countries. Shares of purchased inputs, including fertilizers, tractors, livestock, and irrigation, are also plausible and appear to support the overall underutilization of these resources in different countries. The general insight emerging from this work is that input cost is often a limiting factor for agricultural productivity growth in LAC countries, and the price of labor plays an important role as countries develop.

Other authors have explored the same issue using micro approaches. For example, Solis, Bravo-Ureta, and Quiroga (2009) studied productivity among hillside farmers in El Salvador and Honduras using a household-level, input-oriented stochastic distance frontier. They concluded that differences in the use of purchased inputs (including seeds, fertilizer, pesticides, and hired animal power) explain differences in productivity levels among farmers. Furthermore, purchased inputs have a higher impact on productivity among farmers that use purchased inputs at low levels, suggesting that degree of access to inputs affects productivity growth. These findings are consistent with those of other microlevel studies that have concluded that budget constraints often oblige small-scale farmers to employ suboptimal amounts of inputs. The general conclusion emerging from this work is that access to inputs can significantly affect agricultural productivity growth, and there is a high level of variability in the level of access to inputs in LAC countries.

Extension. Agricultural extension services could be defined as the delivery of information inputs to farmers. These services can play an

BOX 2.1   Does technological change benefit small and large farms equally? Evidence from Mexico

Helfand and Taylor (2016) explore the relationship between farm size and productivity in Mexico and identify factors associated with inefficiency. Earlier work by Kagin, Taylor, and Yuñez-Naude (2016) using data from the Mexico National Rural Household Survey (ENHRUM) found evidence of an inverse relationship between farm size and productivity, driven in part by larger farms being further from the efficiency frontier (that is, smaller farms were more efficient). Using a different data set Mexican Family Life Survey (MxFLS),[a] Helfand and Taylor (2016) expand on the findings by Kagin, Taylor, and Yuñez-Naude by exploring how the relationship may have changed over time.

Helfand and Taylor (2016) find an inverse relationship between farm size and land productivity over the entire range of farm sizes—a relationship that is consistent over time and across samples. In each year, land productivity falls rapidly up to approximately 1 hectare. Around 1 hectare, the relationship levels become relatively flat up to approximately 20 hectares, at which point land productivity once again dramatically declines.

The authors take two complementary approaches to exploring the relationship between farm size and total factor productivity.[b] In the first, they use an average production function to estimate average total factor productivity (TFP). In the second, they use a stochastic production frontier to estimate (1) TFP along the frontier and (2) technical inefficiency, identified as deviations from the frontier. Using the average production function approach, they find a statistically significant inverse relationship between farm size and TFP. Tests of several alternative specifications highlight, however, the need to assume a flexible functional form to fully understand the farm size–productivity relationship because the linear specification does not capture all of the subtleties.

The authors' analysis using the average production function is complemented with analysis using a stochastic production frontier to identify productivity at the technological frontier, as well as the sources of production inefficiencies. The stochastic production frontier approach generates insights into the dynamics of technological change that are difficult to detect using the average production function approach. Alternative specifications of the stochastic production frontier, including some that use survey year dummy variables, generate coefficients that are largely consistent in indicating (1) the existence of a strong inverse relationship between farm size and frontier TFP and (2) the existence of positive technological change—that is, the frontier is increasing over time. The stochastic frontier analysis thus finds positive technological change at the frontier even though, on average, TFP is not observed to rise.

The interactions between farm size and the survey year dummy variables identify a positive and significant relationship between farm size and technological change, suggesting that such change has been biased toward larger farms and that the inverse relationship along the frontier has become less steep over time. Similarly, the interactions between farm size and the survey year dummy variables reveal a dynamic relationship between farm size and technical inefficiency. Although inefficiency has increased over time across the entire farm size distribution, it has increased faster among larger farms. The differential changes in inefficiency across the farm size distribution have caused the farm size–inefficiency relationship to disappear in later waves of the MxFLS.

Helfand and Taylor find that technological change on Mexican farms has been accompanied by increasing technical inefficiency. This finding suggests that the majority of farms have been unable to achieve the same rate of TFP growth as the most productive farms, particularly at the upper end of the farm size distribution. Increasing technical inefficiency resulting from the inability of nonfrontier households to keep up is driving the decline of TFP over time identified in the average production function estimates. These findings are consistent with the time-invariant inverse relationship between farm size and TFP. Along the frontier, the inverse relationship between farm size and productivity is becoming less pronounced because technological advances are favoring larger farms. At the same time, technological advances have been offset by growing inefficiencies among larger farms. Inefficiency was initially smaller for larger farms, but this is no longer true in later waves of the MxFLS. The combination of these two forces has led to a farm size–TFP relationship that has been relatively stable over time.

In summary, the work by Helfand and Taylor (2016) suggests that more rapid technological change at the upper end of the farm size distribution

Box continues next page

BOX 2.1 **Does technological change benefit small and large farms equally? Evidence from Mexico** *(continued)*

indicates an advantage for some larger farms in harnessing more modern agricultural practices. And yet this advantage has not been widespread enough to translate into higher TFP because of the inability of the nonfrontier households to keep up.

a. For more detailed information on the MxFLS composition, longitudinal panel nature of the data, representativeness, and sample size and characteristics refer to Helfand and Taylor (2016). Although not representative of the Mexican agriculture sector per se, the MxFLS is representative of both rural and nonrural Mexican households. Thus use of the data set to study Mexican agriculture must include the important caveat that it likely underrepresents the larger commercial agricultural operations to the degree that they are not family farms. A comparison with the 2007 Agricultural Census reveals that in both the census and MxFLS less than 5 percent of farms are larger than 50 hectares. However, these "large" farms are not necessarily the same as those in the census because they are family-run farms and do not include corporate-run commercial agricultural operations.
b. For details, see annex 1 in Helfand and Taylor (2016).

important role in teaching farmers how to improve their productivity and in moving the products of research—typically information and technical innovations—from the laboratory to the field. Anderson and Feder (2003) argue that productivity improvements are possible only when there is a gap between actual and potential productivity. They describe two types of "gaps" that contribute to the productivity differential: the technology gap and the management gap. Extension can help to reduce the differential between potential and actual yields in farmers' fields by accelerating technology transfer (reducing the technology gap) and by helping farmers become better farm managers (reducing the management gap).

A large empirical literature documents many cases in which extension services have had a measurable impact on agricultural productivity (for summaries, see Alston et al. 2000; Anderson 2007; Birkhaeuser, Evenson, and Feder 1989; Evenson 2000). A practical problem is that most studies have examined the joint impacts of research and extension because the two are often cofinanced and coimplemented. Relatively few studies have assessed the impacts of extension services alone. Generalizing across the empirical literature, it is clear that extension services can significantly accelerate agricultural productivity growth. The effect is not guaranteed, however.

Based on their comprehensive review of the literature, Anderson and Feder (2003) conclude that the record of the impacts of extension on farm performance is actually quite mixed.

Finance. Finance can be used by farmers to bring input levels closer to the optimal level, allowing them to approach the production frontier and increase productivity and production. A large body of empirical evidence from around the world shows that improved access to finance is associated with increased technical efficiency and higher productivity in agriculture. For example, based on a review of more than 30 studies from 14 developing countries, Bravo-Ureta and Pinheiro (1993) concluded that use of credit has a positive and statistically significant impact on technical efficiency at the farm level. Espinoza et al. (2018) used stochastic frontier analysis to explore sources of the variability in farm-level productivity and efficiency in Peru. These authors concluded that access to credit was associated with reduced inefficiency.

Interestingly, although there is abundant evidence that greater access to credit is associated with higher agricultural productivity and production in credit-constrained households, higher agricultural productivity and production do not always translate into higher net income. Carter (1989) found in Nicaragua that, although the use of credit had a positive impact on production, it did not translate into increases in net income measured at market prices.

Education. The positive impact of education on agricultural production and efficiency has been confirmed by many empirical studies. Education improves farmers' decision-making skills and enables them to choose a different mix of inputs and allocate resources more efficiently—the so-called allocative effect. Education also can have a "worker effect" or "technical effect" in which farmers are simply able to use a given amount of resources more efficiently (Reimers and Klasen 2013).

Empirical studies have documented how more years of schooling frequently result in higher levels of agricultural production. Reimers and Klasen (2013) analyzed the impact of education on agricultural productivity across 95 developing countries from 1961 to 2002 and found a 3 percent increase in agricultural productivity for each additional year of schooling.

Risk management. Risk is associated with all production processes, especially in agriculture. Risk stems from uncertainty, which originates in imperfect knowledge. Risk consequently can be thought of as exposure to uncertain consequences that result from imperfect knowledge (Hardaker et al. 2015). In agriculture, imperfect knowledge can apply to many factors, including agroclimatic conditions, market conditions, policy regimes, and the behavior of key players. A large empirical literature has found that risk aversion is common among all groups of farmers, especially among smallholders who have few resources on which to rely in time of production shortfalls. Level of income and various socioeconomic variables typically influence farmers' attitudes to risk, which in turn affect their adoption of technology and therefore productivity. In the absence of well-functioning insurance markets, farmers often have difficulty sharing or pooling risks. As a result, they may choose to invest less (or differently) than they would have done were insurance

available. For example, when farmers face the risk of unpredictable weather or erratic rainfall, they may choose not to invest in high-yielding varieties or fertilizers that could boost agricultural productivity. Using survey data from Honduras, Nicaragua, and Peru, Boucher, Carter, and Guirkinger (2008) show that in the absence of insurance to protect against losses, lenders tend to pass on risk to borrowers, which results in borrowers withdrawing from the credit market. This outcome reduces investment by farmers and negatively affects agricultural productivity.

According to evidence from Latin America, the demand for agricultural insurance is strong, and farmers with access to insurance tend to engage in larger agricultural investments. Moreover, farmers with insurance make riskier production choices than those who do not have insurance—that is, they invest more in the face of uncertainty. Because it gives farmers an incentive to take on more risk, insurance leads to the adoption of technology, resulting in higher productivity and returns over the long run.

Connectivity. The effect of connectivity on agricultural productivity has received more attention in recent years. Helfand and Levine (2004) studied the determinants of productive efficiency in agriculture in Center-West Brazil and found that access to markets facilitated by new infrastructure is an important determinant of agricultural efficiency. Where producers are isolated, transportation-induced transaction costs depress productivity by altering relative prices in such a way that input use is reduced—for evidence from Latin America, see, for example, Goyal and González-Velosa (2012) and Calderón and Servén (2010).

Transportation-induced transaction costs can also affect productivity by influencing crop choice. High transportation costs push farmers to grow food crops that can be stored easily instead of perishable cash crops such as vegetables and fruits that cannot be sold easily in distant markets. Stifel and Minten (2008) found that farmers far from markets grow more low-value staple crops than high-value perishable cash crops. Switching from high-value fruits and vegetables to lower-value cereals and pulses tends to depress agricultural productivity.

Lack of connectivity can also affect agricultural productivity through a third channel—amplifying price variability in isolated areas, thereby forcing farmers to adopt coping mechanisms that lead to lower productivity. In isolated areas where farming households may have few opportunities to diversify their income sources with off-farm activities, farmers who know that prices for agricultural products will be low during the postharvest period and high during the subsequent "hungry season" may insure themselves by expanding production to less fertile land and investing less in inputs, reducing agricultural productivity.

Pushing out the frontier

A second potential source of agricultural productivity growth is expansion of the production possibilities frontier. What are the entry points for helping to push out this frontier, and how effective are they? Two in particular stand out: innovation and education.

Innovation. Innovation that produces changes in technology is a major factor driving technological change leading to TFP growth in agriculture. However, innovation is difficult to define and measure because successful innovation has multiple ingredients, including new technology, an effective technology transfer mechanism, a target population with the requisite knowledge and skills needed to take up the innovation, availability of associated inputs, and favorable economic incentives. Despite the inherently complex nature of innovation, it is clear that a major driver of innovation is research and development (R&D), and the ability of R&D to boost productivity in agriculture has received much attention.

In agriculture, the evidence linking investment in R&D to productivity growth is compelling. Studies comparing the long-term performance of national agriculture sectors have consistently found that countries that invest more in agricultural R&D achieve higher agricultural productivity growth (Craig, Pardey, and Roseboom 1997; Evenson and Fuglie 2009; Evenson and Kislev 1975; Thirtle, Lin, and Piesse 2003). Fuglie et al. (2020) summarize the results of studies that econometrically estimated the impact of R&D on agricultural TFP growth in one or more developing countries. The elasticities appear to show systematic variation in the elasticities of R&D among regions. R&D spillins from national R&D systems of other countries appear to be relatively unimportant for developing countries, unlike in developed countries where cross-country technology transfer has been found to be significant (Fuglie 2018; Schimmelpfennig and Thirtle 1999). A possible explanation is that agricultural R&D in developing countries may be more location-specific (Fuglie 2018). Latin America may be an exception, however. Along with national R&D, international R&D spill-ins and private R&D appear to have made significant contributions to agricultural productivity growth in the LAC region.

Because R&D spending is usually only a small fraction of agricultural GDP, the marginal benefits implied by the elasticities of each dollar of R&D spending tend to be large. Many studies report internal rates of return for public agricultural research spending. They compare costs to benefits, taking into account the lag time between investment in R&D and its effect on productivity. In a meta-analysis of returns to agricultural research, Alston (2010) found that public agricultural research in developing countries earned a median internal rate of return of 39 percent. More recent work by Hurley, Rao, and Pardey (2014) using a modified internal rate of return suggests that although returns have not been as high as had long been reported (median of 9.8 percent a year), they are still substantial.

Education. Education plays a significant role in the adoption and use of technological advances in agricultural production.

Educated farmers are more likely to adopt technology, thereby contributing positively to productivity growth. Specifically, among smallholder rice farmers in Bangladesh an additional year of schooling shifted the rice production frontier by 3–7 percent (Asadullah 2009). Education of farmers not only enhances agricultural productivity following technological adoption as discussed in getting to the frontier, but also promotes adoption itself by creating more informed producers.

More investment in research can have an amplifying effect on agricultural productivity when paired with higher levels of education. Evenson and Fuglie (2009) found that education without improvements in research capacity is not associated with increased productivity growth. Furthermore, in a study of eight East Asian economies Luh, Chang, and Huang (2008) found that domestic R&D and its interaction with human capital have the most significant effects on progress in agricultural technology. This finding suggests that the generation and dissemination of improved technologies should be coupled with farmer education to have a maximum impact on agricultural productivity.

Agricultural growth and poverty reduction

Policy makers are interested in productivity because productivity growth drives growth of the overall economy, resulting in higher incomes, reduced poverty, and improved welfare. In considering the process of structural transformation, which is characterized by shifts in resources between sectors, it is therefore relevant to ask: Does the sector in which growth occurs matter for poverty reduction? This question is especially relevant in developing countries in which a large proportion of the population lives in poverty.

Many empirical studies have concluded that growth in agriculture has been more effective in reducing poverty than growth outside agriculture, especially in closed economies where food is not tradable. The policy relevance of

this finding to a dominant role for agricultural growth in poverty reduction has waned, however. The share of agriculture in most developing economies has declined; economies have become more open as the result of globalization; and food has become more tradable. Many policy makers believe that because productivity in agriculture, especially smallholder agriculture, is now so low compared with productivity in other sectors and because food is sufficiently tradable, poverty reduction is much more likely to come from urbanization. In the LAC region, this view has been reflected in policies designed to facilitate migration out of agriculture, promote industrialization, place greater reliance on food trade, and transform the agriculture sector by introducing mechanized large-scale farming.

This view may not be equally relevant to all countries, however. Recent work summarized in Christiaensen and Martin (2018) suggests that it may not always be correct to assume that when it comes to reducing poverty, growth from any sector has the same effect. Citing results from a coordinated series of studies that used different methodological approaches, the authors argue that growth from agriculture is in general two to three times more effective at reducing poverty than equivalent growth generated outside agriculture. An important caveat, however, is that even though the advantage of agriculture over nonagriculture in reducing poverty is large for the poorest in society, the effect diminishes as incomes rise and ultimately disappears as countries become richer (figure 2.8). The implication is that promoting agricultural growth can be particularly effective as a strategy for reducing poverty in low-income countries, but it will be less effective in middle-income countries and relatively ineffective in high-income countries.

In interpreting this finding that as economies develop and the relatively greater effectiveness of growth from agriculture at reducing poverty declines, it is important to keep in mind that the work summarized by Christiaensen and Martin

FIGURE 2.8 **Effectiveness of growth in different sectors at reducing poverty**

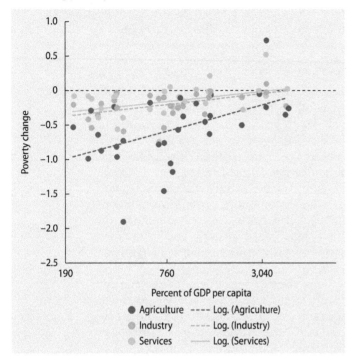

Source: Ivanic and Martin 2018.

(2018) focuses on growth generated only by primary agriculture. To the extent that growth in primary agriculture generates value added and employment through forward and backward linkages, the impacts on poverty reduction would decline more slowly as economies develop. Although it remains uncertain, the fact that as incomes rise the demand increases for processed foods and meals eaten away from home—creating new jobs in the food processing and food services industries—suggests that growth from agriculture may still have a relatively large effect in terms of reducing poverty even in middle- and high-income countries.

Productivity in industry and services

An insight stressed throughout this report is that an important driver of the patterns of structural change observed in the data

for Latin America is the relative pace of productivity growth in the agriculture, industrial, and services sectors. With this in mind, this section evaluates productivity dynamics in industry and services in Latin America, benchmarking it against the dynamics observed in advanced economies and speculating about sources of future growth.

Measuring economic activity is an intrinsically difficult task, even more so when it concerns the services sector. How does one appropriately account for the value added of services that do not operate through a market transaction (government services, the digital economy)? What types of business services are offered in Latin America compared with those in more advanced economies? Are they similar? Because of the increasing participation of the services sector in aggregate production, the consequences of these challenges are even more pronounced.

Another layer of difficulty lies in the lack of data needed to compute total factor productivity by sector and across countries. The main data source used for this type of analysis, the Groningen Growth and Development Centre's 10-Sector Database, offers internationally comparable data on real value added and employment, making it suitable for the task of measuring labor productivity. However, it does not offer information on sectoral capital stocks. Hereafter, then, every reference to sectoral productivity will refer to the dynamics of labor productivity.

Labor productivity in services and industry: Latin America and the United States

A natural starting point for assessing the performance of Latin America in terms of the productivity growth of its industrial and services sector is to compare it with the performance of advanced economies.

The first step is to evaluate the productivity dynamics of sectors individually. Are sectors in the LAC region catching up with the global frontier or lagging further? In the second step, because this relative pace of growth guides the sectoral allocation of resources in theory, it is instructive to contrast the performance of Latin America and the United States in terms of the relative growth of the productivity of the industrial and services sectors.

Figure 2.9 reports the dynamics of labor productivity in the industrial and services sectors for Latin America and the United States between 1950 and 2010, measured as value added per worker. The salient property of the figure is that, although there is some evidence of convergence in industrial productivity, the performance of the services sector in Latin America is worsening relative to that of the United States. Chile and Brazil, the best performers, managed to outpace the United States in terms of industrial productivity growth, indicative of convergence. However, even for these best performers of the region, the pace of productivity growth in the services sector could not keep up with productivity growth in the United States. Surprisingly

disappointing is the performance of Mexico, especially after 1980, when a healthy pace of technological upgrading in both sectors was interrupted, leaving it on track to be one of the worst performers in the region. The most worrisome case is Bolivia, whose level of productivity declined over the course of six decades.

The underperformance of many of Latin America's services sectors is also worrisome in view of the fast pace of deindustrialization in the region. Although there is scope for slowing down deindustrialization by addressing the distortions that underlie it, the prospects of sustaining growth accelerations in the region becomes grimmer because the lower pace of productivity growth in services precipitates the reallocation of economic activity toward that slow-growing sector. In short, a reversal of the disappointing rate of growth in the services sectors will play an important role in Latin America moving up from its designation as a sticky, low-middle-income region.

FIGURE 2.9 **Labor productivity growth in industrial and services sectors: Latin America and United States, 1950–2010**

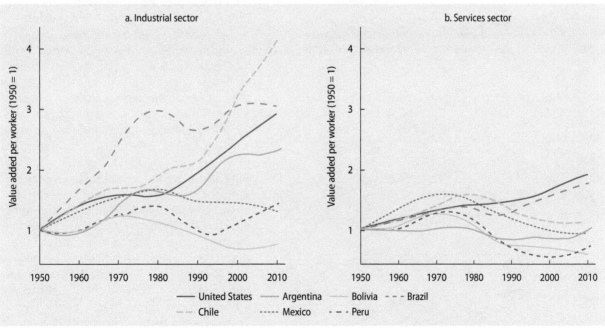

Source: Fattal Jaef 2019.

Relative prices: Relative productivity growth between services and industry

Evaluation of the productivity dynamics of each sector independently is useful to fully appreciate that underwhelming productivity growth is a widespread phenomenon in Latin America. In terms of helping understand structural change, however, it is the relative pace of productivity growth between sectors that acts as a driving force. For this reason, figure 2.10 illustrates how Latin America has fared in relation to the United States in terms of the pace of the relative productivity growth of the industrial and services sectors.

Although it is a shared feature of almost every country that productivity growth in industry outpaces services, this pattern is most pronounced in Latin America. Interpreted from standard theories of structural change, this relative decline in services sector productivity is a primary driver of a reallocation of economic activity toward that sector. It is this driving force, combined with the lethargic pace of productivity growth in services, that substantiates the concern about long-term growth in the region.

Sources of productivity growth: The potential of improving allocative efficiency

One way or the other, every evaluation of the long-term behavior of an economy ends up discussing the conceivable drivers of productivity growth. How will Latin America improve the productivity of its services sector? Among the long list of candidates is the role of allocative efficiency, which is the focus here. What is the scope in Latin America for raising total factor productivity by means of allocating productive resources more efficiently across firms?

The justification for focusing on misallocation lies primarily in that it not only constitutes a conceptually plausible source of productivity growth in the future, but also has been shown to constitute a barrier to productivity growth in many economies. Because most studies focus on manufacturing productivity, it is useful to revisit the literature and uncover findings on misallocation in the services sector, especially in Latin America.

To appreciate the mechanisms through which resource misallocation harms total factor productivity, consider the following scenario. Two producers, A and B, provide an identical service, albeit using different technology. For a given number of hours worked, producer A can supply more units of the service than producer B. Subject to diminishing marginal products, the output maximizing rule will allocate workers across firms until their marginal products are equalized. Because producer A is more productive than producer B, A will ultimately operate a larger firm. Now suppose a distortion in the economy interferes with the efficient rule. For example, bigger firms may be subjected to higher tax rates than smaller firms. This policy would discourage producer A from achieving an efficient size and force a cut in the labor force to below the optimal level. Despite some wage adjustment because of the excess supply of labor, the equilibrium

FIGURE 2.10 **Labor productivity in services sector relative to industrial sector: Latin America and United States, 1950–2010**

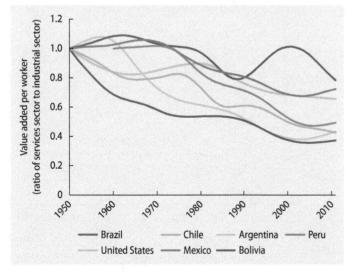

Source: Fattal Jaef 2019.

allocation will result in fewer workers for producer A and more for producer B. Because of the productivity differences across producers, and for a given size of the labor force, lower output will be the outcome in the aggregate.

The logic just described provides a strategy for measuring the degree of misallocation in a country. Specifically, efficient allocation carries the strong testable implication that, among comparable goods and services (for example, in the same four-digit Standard Industrial Classification industry code), the value of marginal products across firms should be equalized. Otherwise, workers could be reallocated toward high marginal product firms and increase the aggregate amount of output. Therefore, a sufficient statistic of the degree of misallocation in a narrow industry or sector is the standard deviation of the marginal revenue products. Because of the increasing availability of firm-level data sets, it is now possible to measure the deviation between actual and efficient allocation from the data.

How pervasive is misallocation in industry and services?

Bowing to data constraints, most of the literature on misallocation focuses on manufacturing industries. The evidence thus far provides compelling evidence that misallocation is prevalent in the developing world and is preventing these economies from reaping substantial gains in TFP. Table 2.1 summarizes the statistics on misallocation for several countries in Latin America and Sub-Saharan Africa, alongside the counterfactual gains in TFP that would accrue if the efficient allocation were to be implemented. As a baseline, the table also shows misallocation for the United States.[2]

The main message conveyed by the table is that the manufacturing misallocation in Latin America is almost as severe as it is in China, India, and many Sub-Saharan economies, and the potential TFP gains from reverting misallocation to the US level range

between 10 percentage points (Chile) and 50 percentage points (Mexico).

This report takes on the question of what countries could do to alleviate misallocation. In the meantime, it is instructive to recall that if countries were to find a way to reap the gains from reversing misallocation, the subsequent growth in industrial productivity would, unless accompanied by an equal or stronger force in services sector productivity growth, result in a deepening of the reallocation of employment toward the services sector. On the one hand, growth in industrial productivity increases aggregate income. Through income effects, expenditure moves away from agriculture to industry and services. On the other hand, the relative price channel, directly connected to the widening of the gap in productivity growth between industry and the services sector, further contributes to the reallocation of employment to the services sector. Therefore, the

TABLE 2.1 **Misallocation in manufacturing, selected developing and developed countries**

Country	Standard deviation, revenue productivity	TFP gain, efficient allocation (%)
United States	0.49	42.9
China	0.63	86.6
India	0.67	127.5
Colombia	1.21	50.5
Venezuela, R.B.	1.28	64.7
El Salvador	0.64	60.6
Chile	0.72	53.8
Uruguay	0.97	60.2
Bolivia	0.88	60.6
Ecuador	0.62	57.6
Argentina	0.62	60.0
Mexico	0.82	95.0
Ethiopia	0.78	66.6
Ghana	0.95	75.7
Kenya	1.52	162.6
Côte d'Ivoire	0.65	31.4

Sources: Data, United States, India, and China: Hsieh and Klenow (2009); Sub-Saharan Africa: Cirera, Fattal-Jaef, and Hibret Maemir (2020).
Note: TFP = total factor productivity.

degree to which the reversal of misallocation will contribute to structural transformation hinges critically on the pattern of misallocation in the services sector.

What about misallocation in services? The evidence here is much thinner. Representative firm-level data sets on services sectors are scarcer than they are for manufacturing, constituting the main hurdle for achieving a comparable density of research. Furthermore, the inherent difficulties in measuring the value added of various services make measurement of misallocation more prone to measurement error, thereby hindering its validity as a useful diagnostic tool.

Still, based on the existing inquiries into the role of misallocation in services, the conclusion is that distortions in the services sector seem to be more prevalent and damaging than they are for the industrial sector. Dias, Marques, and Richmond (2019) estimated misallocation and the associated counterfactual TFP gains from its resolution in Portugal's economy between 1996 and 2011. They found that the potential for TFP growth through efficient reallocation is about twice as large in the services sector as in the industrial sector.

A similar quantification was performed by Garcia-Santana et al. (2016) for Spain's economy between 1995 and 2007. In this case, the construction sector exhibited the lowest allocative efficiency, but again misallocation was worse in the services sector than in the industrial sector.

The conclusion about the relative severity of misallocation in services versus industry was also confirmed in the Latvian economy during the financial crisis and its aftermath, as reported by Benkovskis (2015).

Turning to Latin America, the evidence is confined to a study by Crespi, Tacsir, and Vargas (2016). The authors perform a more general investigation of the drivers of the low level of productivity in Latin America. A factor here, however, is that the methodology for the characterization of misallocation underpinning the work by Crespi, Tacsir, and Vargas (2016) is different from that used in the studies summarized

so far. In those studies, misallocation is measured as deviations from a theoretically prescribed benchmark of efficiency, as in the pioneering work of Hsieh and Klenow (2009). Crespi, Tacsir, and Vargas (2016) base the indicator of allocative efficiency on Olley and Pakes (1996), which measures allocative efficiency as the degree of correlation between the value-added share of a firm and its relative productivity with respect to that of the average firm in its industry.

Even using a different methodology, the study by Crespi, Tacsir, and Vargas (2016) confirms that allocative efficiency in Latin America is lower in the services sector than in the industrial sector. This evidence points once again to distortions in the business environment that have a disproportionate effect on firms in the services sector. This distinction is important in thinking about what type of friction or policy may be behind the observed misallocation. For example, if credit market frictions are the culprit, then it must be that external finance dependence is more prevalent in services than in industry. Another candidate is state-owned enterprises, which tend to be more common among services.

Taking stock: The scope for raising allocative efficiency and the expected pace of structural change

This chapter has revealed that there is scope in Latin America for raising total factor productivity by improving the allocative efficiency in an economy. Furthermore, a review of the existing evidence points toward a higher prevalence of misallocation in the services sector than in the industrial sector. To connect back to the primary objective of this study, structural change, what is the implication of the observed misallocation for the future pattern of sectoral resource allocation?

Answering the question requires going back to the fundamental drivers of structural change in a country. As discussed earlier in the presentation of the theoretical framework, these drivers stem from the incentives to move expenditures toward income elastic goods and services as countries become richer and the incentives to reallocate resources toward sectors with relatively lower productivity growth.

The fact that misallocation is severer in services than in industry implies that there is a channel through which productivity in services will catch up with productivity in the industrial sector. In the short to medium term, as misallocation is progressively reversed, theory implies that deindustrialization will slow and aggregate growth will go up. In the long run, however, once the gains from efficient reallocation have been reaped, the pace of deindustrialization and the long-run growth in the economy will again be determined by the long-run forces driving productivity growth in each sector. Unless the resolution of misallocation translates into a permanent change in the rate of technological progress, the boost in industrial activity and aggregate growth will be temporary.

This permanent effect of dismantling misallocation on productivity growth is not an unreasonable possibility. It is quite possible that, once firms are confronted with distortions that damage their profitability, not only will resources flow out of the most productive firms (static misallocation effect), but also firms will be more reluctant to invest in innovations that would make them even more productive (dynamic effect through innovation).

In short, at the very least the current relatively low levels of allocative efficiency in the services sector are an opportunity to slow down the deindustrialization of Latin American economies and boost aggregate growth. The perpetuation of these trends will depend to a large extent on the credibility of the reforms that are implemented to boost allocative efficiency and that would induce firms to innovate and invest in technology.

The future in manufacturing

The new technologies of the so-called Fourth Industrial Revolution are threatening the potential for large-scale industrialization in developing countries. Specifically, the introduction of new labor-saving technologies is reducing the importance of low wages as a determinant of comparative advantage. In other words, labor costs are becoming less important, whereas quality, reduced time to market, faster innovation, and scale economies are becoming more relevant.

New technologies are enabling suppliers to produce higher-quality goods at lower prices, and thus suppliers using older technologies will need to adapt or they will not survive. However, the adoption of new technologies requires complementary investments in infrastructure (particularly in ICT technologies) and human capital, as well as modernization of the regulatory system to address issues of intellectual property, privacy, and ownership of data. Meanwhile, the expectation is that global value chains (GVCs) will shorten, and there will likely be fewer entry points in the future (Hallward-Driemeier and Nayyar 2018).

In their book, Hallward-Driemeier and Nayyar (2018) analyze in detail the feasibility of expanding production by industrial subsector. In their analysis, they consider aspects such as the relative magnitude of automation (measured by the density of robots per 1,000 workers), export concentration, service intensity, and the extent to which goods in a subsector are internationally traded. What follows are the two conclusions most relevant to the LAC economies.

First, despite the changing globalization patterns and the emergence of new labor-saving technologies, in some manufacturing industries there is room for insertion or expansion. Examples are commodity-based processing manufacturers that are less automated, less concentrated in terms of export locations, and less intensive in the use of professional services. Also, for industries such as textiles, garments, and footwear, which are labor-intensive and tradable, countries with low unit labor costs may retain a comparative advantage. There also may be scope to serve domestic or regional markets for lower-quality, lower-price manufactures across industries.

Second, Hallward-Driemeier and Nayyar highlight the potentially negative effects of *not* adopting new technologies. If new production methods in traded goods render higher-quality goods at lower prices, domestic production using older technologies may not be able to compete. This may result in fewer jobs created or even job losses. Therefore, firms may need to adopt new technologies just to remain globally competitive. The authors conclude that "manufacturing will likely continue to deliver on productivity, scale, trade, and innovation, but just not with the same number of jobs. So, its unique desirability in terms of the twin wins of productivity and jobs is eroding."

The future in services

The traditional view generally holds services as an inferior sector that has low productivity and, perhaps more important, lower productivity growth. As a result, the structural transformation process that increases the importance of the services sector appears to be terrible news for the region because it implies a slowdown of aggregate productivity growth. This is known in the economic literature as Baumol's disease.

Taken as a whole, the services sector does appear to have lower productivity growth than the industrial sector. However, the services sector is composed of a very diverse set of subsectors that differ significantly in their productivity levels, in their productivity growth, and even in their use of skilled labor. In fact, a more disaggregated view of the services sector reveals huge heterogeneity in which some subsectors are more productive and skill-intensive than manufacturing. Specifically, there is evidence that service industries that are intensive in knowledge, ICT, and trade, such as telecommunications, finance, and logistics. have higher rates of productivity growth than manufacturing (Jorgenson and Timmer 2011). In fact, recent evidence suggests that there is unconditional convergence; countries with lower initial labor productivity

in the services sector grow faster than those with higher initial labor productivity in that sector (Enache, Ghani, and O'Connell 2016; Kinfemichael and Morshed 2016). Moreover, Fagerberg and Verspagen (2002) suggest that the services sector has increasingly contributed to economic growth over the last 30 years.

These results are related to the fact that the services sector is increasingly sharing pro-development characteristics that were once thought of as the unique domain of manufacturing. The huge advances in ICT technologies have enabled the emergence of service subsectors—financial, telecommunications, and business services—that can be digitally stored, codified, and more easily traded (Ghani and Kharas 2010). Meanwhile, the deregulation of services markets has been accompanied by large inflows of foreign direct investment. Therefore, certain service subsectors are looking more and more like the manufacturing sector, with exposure to trade and inflows of FDI allowing greater competition, technology diffusion, and the benefits of scale.

It is important to note, however, that these service subsectors, which can substantially contribute to increasing productivity, are also highly skill-intensive. Thus their capacity to provide employment for unskilled labor may be limited. However, some service subsectors are intensive in the use of unskilled labor. Unfortunately, these subsectors are generally low-productivity growth sectors and thus will contribute less to aggregate productivity.

As noted earlier, Baumol's disease refers to the phenomenon in which structural change slows down aggregate productivity growth when it reallocates production to industries with low productivity growth—see, for example, Baumol (1967); Nordhaus (2008); and Oulton (2001). The question that follows is whether in the future these industries will gradually take over the economy and drive down aggregate productivity growth. In a recent paper, Duernecker, Herrendorf, and Valentinyi (2017) add a novel feature to the standard structural transformation model; specifically, they disaggregate the services sector into services with high productivity growth and services with low productivity growth. This approach is a deviation from the literature, which typically considers one broad services sector and abstracts from the heterogeneity in service industries. Although the model by Duernecker, Herrendorf, and Valentinyi (2017). generates the usual structural change between the goods and services sectors, it also implies structural change within the services sector itself. They find that for the postwar United States the calibration of the utility function implies that services with low productivity growth are luxuries, high-productivity services are necessities, and the two service subsectors are substitutes. This substitutability between the two service subsectors limits the importance of the low-productivity subsector in the economy and thus the future productivity effects of Baumol's disease.

Blurring lines

Another important trend worth noting is the "servicification" of manufacturing. This term refers to the fact that manufacturing firms are not only integrating more services into their production function, but also selling and exporting more services as integrated activities. It is useful to distinguish these two aspects of servicification. On the one hand, the increasing use of services as inputs in the production process is described as services *embodied* in goods. On the other hand, *embedded* services are those that are bundled with the goods provided to customers, such as sales and after-sales services.

These services are increasingly accounting for much of the value added in a product's supply chain. Stan Shih, Acer's CEO during the 1990s, has described the relationship between the stages of production and the contribution to total value added as a "smiley curve." Essentially, he is referring to the fact that upstream activities such as product design and R&D and downstream activities such as branding and advertising services contribute a large share of total value added, while the intermediate production stages contribute the least.

As noted earlier, the productivity of services used as inputs in production (such as for design and marketing) or as enablers for trade (such as logistics and e-commerce platforms) are essential to the competitiveness and growth of the industrial sector. The estimates of Sinha (2019a) suggest that if distortions of services as intermediate goods (embodied services) had been kept at their historical minimum, the industrial sector would have been 2–2.5 percentage points larger as a share of the economy. Moreover, the value added of embodied services, specially distribution and business services, have contributed more than a third of the value of gross manufacturers' exports globally (Hallward-Driemeier and Nayyar 2018). According to a growing body of evidence, this servicification of manufacturing has raised manufacturing productivity in the Czech Republic, India, and Sub-Saharan Africa (Arnold, Javorcik, and Mattoo 2011; Arnold, Mattoo, and Narciso 2008).

Recent literature has highlighted the key role of services as a supplier of inputs to the rest of the economy. In fact, Alvarez et al. (2019) find that in the LAC region this sector has the highest degree of forward linkages and the highest degree of influence. Moreover, they find that if several subsectors in services—such as business services, trade, and transport—closed their productivity gap relative to the Organisation for Economic Co-operation and Development (OECD) average, it would generate the greatest contribution to aggregate productivity.

Conclusions and policy implications

This chapter has reviewed productivity performance and dynamics by sector. Although agricultural productivity has increased in the LAC region, there is still room for further improvement. Two main avenues for productivity growth are (1) improving the technical efficiency of producers using existing technology and (2) pushing out the production possibilities frontier by shifting to new, improved technologies.

As for the industrial sector—specifically, the manufacturing subsector—the evidence clearly shows that there is a substantial degree of misallocation between firms. The firm-size distribution is skewed toward small and microenterprises. This finding points toward distortions in the market that are preventing the consolidation and growth of the most productive firms. Thus governments need to institute policies that foster competition—such as international trade and deepening of regional trade agreements. Revisions are needed as well of size-dependent policies (or enforcement) that appear to hamper the growth of productive firms and incentivize informality.

The future of further industrialization is subject to growing requirements for complementary infrastructure, technology absorption capacity, and workforce skills. Increasingly, firms will need to adopt new technologies just to stay competitive. The introduction of new labor-saving technologies is reducing the importance of low wages as a determinant of comparative advantage. Instead, quality, reduced time to market, faster innovation, and scale economies are becoming more relevant. Moreover, emerging technologies (such as 3D printing) are expected to shorten global value chains, limiting the opportunities for entry. Therefore, opportunities for further industrialization (or reindustrialization) may be more limited and subject to higher requirements in the future.

Urgently needed are a comprehensive set of policy actions to address productivity issues in the services sector. The sector already employs more than 60 percent of the workforce in the LAC region, and current trends indicate that it will continue to grow and be the main source of job creation in the future. Although the scarcity

of data on the services sector is an obstacle to a clearer diagnosis, the existing evidence indicates that there is a higher degree of misallocation in this sector relative to manufacturing.

Governments should also focus on increasing competition in the services sector by removing distortions in the market and by opening these sectors to international trade. Figure 2.11 shows the results of applying the Services Trade Restrictions Index to nine LAC countries.[3] The index measures the degree to which countries are open to international trade in five service subsectors: telecommunications, financial, transportation, retail, and professional services. A score of zero indicates that the country is completely open, and a score of 100 implies that it is completely closed. For the region, it appears that telecommunications and professional services are the most restricted sectors, whereas transportation is also relevant for some countries.

Recent literature suggests that the services sector is heavily intertwined with the rest of the economy and is the most important sector in terms of being a supplier of inputs. In addition, the recent trend of "servicification" of manufacturing implies that more services are being used as inputs in the production of goods (embodied services) and more services are provided to customers bundled with the goods (embedded services). Therefore, the increased productivity of backbone services—such as logistics, ICT, and business services—could ripple throughout the economy, having larger impacts on overall aggregate productivity. In fact, as noted, Sinha (2019b) finds that reductions in the cost of service inputs could have quantitatively important effects on the size of the industrial sector.

Figure 2.12 presents the performance of LAC countries relative to the global best performer on the Logistics Performance Index.[4] It shows that there is significant room for improvement across all countries in the LAC region. In particular, the region can significantly improve on the

FIGURE 2.11   **Services Trade Restrictions Index, selected LAC countries**

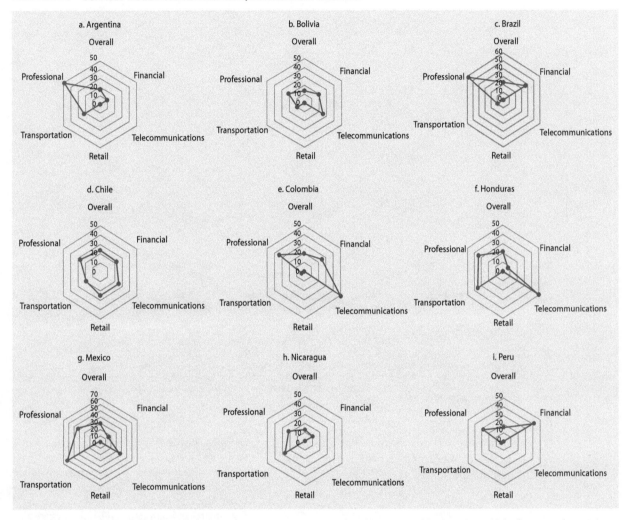

Source: Original calculations for this publication using World Bank's Services Trade Restrictions Database (https://www.worldbank.org/en/research/brief/services-trade-restrictions
-database).
Note: The graphs depict information on five sectors: financial, telecommunications, retail, transportation, and professional services. All datapoints were collected in 2008,
except for Mexico and Brazil (2011). The quantitative interpretation of the numbers is as follows: open without restrictions (0 points); virtually open (25 points); existence of
major/nontrivial restrictions (50 points); virtually closed (75 points); completely closed (100 points); LAC = Latin America and the Caribbean.

customs, infrastructure, and logistics quality components.

Therefore, policy makers in the LAC region should focus on productivity growth and not on the size of any one economic sector. There is room for improvement in all sectors of the economy, but a dedicated reform agenda is urgently needed for the services sector. Resources should be invested in data collection to better understand the specific issues affecting the productivity of firms in this sector. Because of

the size of the sector, the expectation that it will continue to grow, its higher degree of misallocation (relative to the industrial sector), and its role as input provider to the rest of the economy, the productivity agenda for the services sector should be a priority for policy makers in the region.

As for the future generally, the structure of the LAC economy is changing, and the requirements for productivity growth within sectors are increasing. In particular, the demand for skills is changing. What are the

FIGURE 2.12   Logistics Performance Index and its components: 16 LAC countries, relative to best performer

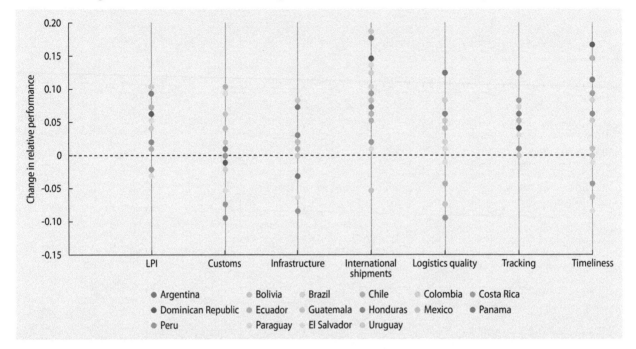

Source: Original calculations for this publication using World Bank's Logistics Performance Index, 2018 (https://lpi.worldbank.org/) for LAC economies.
Note: All values indicate the relative score of any given economy using Germany as a benchmark. *LPI* refers to the composite Logistics Performance Index; *customs* refers to the efficiency of customs and borders clearance; *infrastructure* refers to the quality of trade and transport infrastructure; *international shipments* refers to the ease of arranging competitively priced shipments; *tracking* refers to the ability to track and trace consignments; *timeliness* refers to the frequency with which scheduled or expected delivery arrives within expected delivery times; LAC = Latin America and the Caribbean.

implications of these changes for jobs and the future of work? The next chapter turns to these questions.

Notes

1. Agriculture refers to the production from crops, livestock, forestry, and fisheries.
2. The expectation is that misallocation should be close to zero in the United States, presumably an undistorted economy. Table 2.1 reveals that there is indeed misallocation in the US economy, albeit to a lesser degree. Noting that part of what the methodology captures as misallocation could arise from measurement error, one could crudely control for measurement error by attributing all the misallocation in the United States to measurement error and subtracting the US numbers from those of the rest of the countries. In other words, only the dispersion in revenue productivity in excess of the dispersion in the United States is actual misallocation. Likewise, only the TFP gains

in excess of the US gains are the actual gains from resolving misallocation. This method would control only for the measurement error that does not vary systematically across countries.

3. For more information on the index, see https://www.worldbank.org/en/research/brief /services-trade-restrictions-database.
4. For more information on the index, see https://lpi.worldbank.org/about.

References

Alston, J. M. 2010. "The Benefits from Agricultural Research and Development, Innovation, and Productivity Growth." OECD Food, Agriculture and Fisheries Paper No. 31, OECD Publishing, Paris.

Alston, J. M., C. Chan-Kang, M. C. Marra, P. G. Pardey, and T. J. Wyatt. 2000. "A Meta-analysis of Rates of Return to Agricultural R&D: Ex Pede Herculem?" Research Report Vol. 113, International Food Policy Research Institute, Washington, DC.

Álvarez, F., Eslava, M., Sanguinetti, P., Toledo, M., Eslava, M., Alves, G., and others. 2019. *RED 2018: Institutions for Productivity: Towards a Better Business Environment.* Caracas: CAF. http://scioteca.caf.com/handle123456789/1410.

Anderson, J. R. 2007. "Agricultural Advisory Services." Background paper, *World Development Report 2008.* http://siteresources.worldbank.orglINTWDR2008I Resources/2795087119142798678S/Anderson_AdvisoryServices.pdf.

Anderson, J. R., and G. Feder. 2003. "Rural Extension Services." Policy Research Working Paper 2976, World Bank, Washington, DC.

Arnold, J. M., B. S. Javorcik, and A. Mattoo. 2011. "Does Services Liberalization Benefit Manufacturing Firms? Evidence from the Czech Republic." *Journal of International Economics* 85 (1): 136–46.

Arnold, J. M., A. Mattoo, and G. Narciso. 2008. "Services Inputs and Finn Productivity in Sub-Saharan Africa: Evidence from Firm-Level Data." *Journal of African Economies* 17 (4): 578–99.

Asadullah, M. N. 2009. "Returns to Private and Public Education in Bangladesh and Pakistan: A Comparative Analysis." *Journal of Asian Economics* 20 (1): 77–86.

Assunção, J. J., and L. H. Braido. 2007. "Testing Household-Specific Explanations for the Inverse Productivity Relationship." *American Journal of Agricultural Economics* 89 (4): 980–90.

Barrett, C. B. 1996. "On Price Risk and the Inverse Farm Size-Productivity Relationship." *Journal of Development Economics* 51 (2): 193–215.

Barrett, C. B., M. F. Bellemare, and J. Y. Hou. 2010. "Reconsidering Conventional Explanations of the Inverse Productivity-Size Relationship." *World Development* 38 (1): 88–97.

Baumol, W. J. 1967. "Macroeconomics of Unbalanced Growth: The Anatomy of Urban Crisis." *American Economic Review* 57 (3): 415–26.

Benjamin, D. 1992. "Household Composition, Labor Markets, and Labor Demand: Testing for Separation in Agricultural Household Models." *Econometrica: Journal of the Econometric Society* 60 (2): 287–322.

Benkovskis, K. 2015. "Misallocation of Resources in Latvia: Did Anything Change during the Crisis?" Working paper, Bank of Latvia, Riga.

Birkhaeuser, D., R. E. Evenson, and G. Feder. 1989. "The Economic Impact of Agricultural Extension: A Review." Center Discussion Paper No. 567, Yale Economic Growth Center, New Haven, CT.

Bolt, J., R. Inklaar, H. de Jong, and J. Luiten van Zanden. 2018. "Rebasing 'Maddison': New Income Comparisons and the Shape of Long-run Economic Development." Maddison Project Working Paper 10, Groningen Growth and Development Centre (GGDC), Groningen, The Netherlands.

Boucher S. R., M. R. Carter, and K. Guirkinger. 2008. "Risk Rationing and Wealth Effects in Credit Markets-Theory and Implications for Agricultural Development." *American Journal for Agricultural Economics* 90 (2): 409–23.

Bravo-Ureta, B., and A. Pinheiro. 1993. "Efficiency Analysis of Developing Country Agriculture: A Review of the Frontier Function Literature." *Agricultural and Resource Economics Review* 22 (1): 88–101.

Calderón, C., and L. Servén. 2010. *Infrastructure in Latin America.* Washington, DC: World Bank.

Carletto, G., S. Savastano, and A. Zezza. 2013. "Fact or Artifact: The Impact of Measurement Errors on the Farm Size-Productivity Relationship." *Journal of Development Economics* 103: 254–61.

Carter, M. R 1989. "The Impact of Credit on Peasant Productivity and Differentiation in Nicaragua." *Journal of Development Economics* 31 (1): 13–36.

Christiaensen, L., and W. Martin. 2018. *Agriculture, Structural Transformation and Poverty Reduction: Eight New Insights.* Amsterdam: Elsevier.

Cirera, X., R. Fattal-Jaef, and H. Maemir. 2020. "Taxing the Good? Distortions, Misallocation, and Productivity in Sub-Saharan Africa," *World Bank Economic Review 34 (1): 75-100.* World Bank Group, Washington, DC.

Coelli, T. J., and D. P. Rao. 2003. "Total Factor Productivity Growth in Agriculture: A Malmquist Index Analysis of 93 Countries, 1980–2000." Draft paper, University of Queensland, Brisbane.

Craig, B. J., P. G. Pardey, and J. Roseboom. 1997. "International Productivity Patterns: Accounting for Input Quality, Infrastructure, and Research." *American Journal of Agricultural Economics* 79 (4): 1064–76.

Crespi, G., E. Tacsir, and F. Vargas. 2016. "Innovation Dynamics and Productivity: Evidence for Latin America." In *Firm Innovation and Productivity in Latin America and the Caribbean,* 37–71. New York: Palgrave Macmillan.

Dias, D. A, C. Robalo Marques, and C. Richmond. 2019. "A Tale of Two Sectors: Why Is Misallocation Higher in Services than in Manufacturing?" *Review of Income and Wealth,* April 3.

Duernecker, G., B. Herrendorf, and A. K. Valentinyi. 2017. "Structural Change within the Service Sector and the Future of Baumol's Disease." Centre for Economic Policy Research, London.

Eastwood, R., M. Lipton, and A. Newell. 2010. "Farm Size." *Handbook of Agricultural Economics* 4: 3323–97.

Enache, M., E. Ghani, and S. O'Connell. 2016. "Structural Transformation in Africa: A Historical View." Policy Research Working Paper 7743, World Bank, Washington, DC.

Espinoza, M., R. Fort, M. Morris, A. Sebastian, and L. Villazón. 2018. "Understanding Heterogeneity in Peruvian Agriculture: A Meta-Frontier Approach for Analyzing Technical Efficiency." Paper presented to the 2018 Conference of International Association of Agricultural Economists, July 28–August 2, Vancouver, BC.

Eswaran, M., and A. Kotwal. 1989. "Credit as Insurance in Agrarian Economies." *Journal of Development Economics* 1 (1): 37–53.

Evenson, R E. 2000. "How Far Away Is Africa? Technological Spillovers to Agriculture and Productivity." *American Journal of Agricultural Economics* 82 (3): 743–49.

Evenson, R. E., and K. Fuglie. 2009. "Technology Capital: The Price of Admission to the Growth Club." *Journal of Productivity Analysis* 33 (3): 173–90.

Evenson, R. E., and Y. Kislev. 1975. *Agricultural Research and Productivity.* New Haven, CT: Yale University Press.

Fagerberg, J., and B. Verspagen. 2002. "Technology-Gaps, Innovation-Diffusion and Transformation: An Evolutionary Interpretation." *Research Policy* 31 (8-9): 1291–304.

Fattal Jaef, R. 2019. "Quantitative Evaluation of the Premature Deindustrialization Hypothesis in Latin America?" Working paper, World Bank, Washington, DC.

Feder, G. 1985. "The Relation between Farm Size and Farm Productivity: The Role of Family Labor, Supervision and Credit Constraints." *Journal of Development Economics* 18 (2–3): 297–313.

Fuglie, K. P. 2015. "Accounting for Growth in Global Agriculture." *Bio-Based and Applied Economics* 4 (3): 201–34.

Fuglie, K. P. 2018. "R&D Capital, R&D Spillovers, and Productivity Growth in World Agriculture." *Applied Economic Perspectives and Policy* 40 (3): 421–44.

Fuglie, K. P., M. Gautam, A. Goyal, and W. F. Maloney. 2020. *Harvesting Prosperity Technology and Productivity Growth in Agriculture.* Washington, DC: World Bank.

Fuglie, K. P., P. Heisey, J. King, C. Pray, and D. Schimmelpfennig. 2012. "The Contribution of Private Industry to Agricultural Innovation." *Science,* November 23, 1031–32.

García-Santana, M., E. Moral-Benito, J. Pijoan-Mas, and R. Ramos. 2016. "Growing Like Spain: 1995–2007." Working Paper 16098, Bank of Spain, Madrid.

Ghani, E., and H. Kharas. 2010. "The Service Revolution." Brief 54595, World Bank, Washington, DC.

Goyal, A., and C. González-Velosa. 2012. "Improving Agricultural Productivity and Market Efficiency in Latin America and the Caribbean: How ICTs Can Make a Difference?" Working Paper 68255, World Bank, Washington, DC.

Hallward-Driemeier, M., and G. Nayyar. 2018. *Trouble in the Making? The Future of Manufacturing-led Development.* Washington, DC: World Bank.

Hardaker J. B., G. Lien, J. R. Anderson, and R. B. M. Huirne. 2015. *Coping with Risk in Agriculture: Applied Decision Analysis,* 3rd ed. Wallingford, UK: Centre for Agriculture and Bioscience International.

Helfand, S. M., and E. S. Levine. 2004. "Farm Size and the Determinants of Productive Efficiency in the Brazilian Center-West." *Agricultural Economics* 31 (2–3): 241–49.

Helfand, S. M., and M. Taylor. 2016. "Agricultural Productivity and Farm Size in Latin America." University of California, Riverside.

Hsieh, C.-T., and P. J. Klenow. 2009. "Misallocation and Manufacturing TFP in China and India." *Quarterly Journal of Economics* 124 (4): 1403–48.

Hurley, T. M., X. Rao, and P. G. Pardey. 2014. "Re-examining the Reported Rates of Return to Food and Agricultural Research and

Development." *American Journal of Agricultural Economics* 96 (5): 1492–04.

Ivanic, M., and W. Martin. 2018. "Sectoral Productivity Growth and Poverty Reduction: National and Global Impacts." *World Development* 109: 429–39.

Jorgenson, D. W., and M. P. Timmer. 2011. "Structural Change in Advanced Nations: A New Set of Stylised Facts." *Scandinavian Journal of Economics* 113 (1): 1–29.

Kagin, J., J. E. Taylor, and A. Yuñez-Naude. 2016. "Inverse Productivity or Inverse Efficiency? Evidence from Mexico." *Journal of Development Studies* 52 (3): 396–411.

Kinfemichael, B., and A. M. Morshed. 2016. "Convergence of Labor Productivity across the US States." *Economic Modeling* 76 (C): 270–80.

Luh, Y. H., C. Chang, and F. Huang. 2008. "Efficiency Change and Productivity Growth in Agriculture: A Comparative Analysis for Selected East Asian Economies." *Journal of Asian Economics* 19 (4): 312–24.

Nordhaus, W. D. 2008. "Baumol's Diseases: A Macroeconomic Perspective." *BE Journal of Macroeconomics* 8 (1).

Olley, G., and A. Pakes. 1996. "The Dynamics of Productivity in the Telecommunications Equipment Industry." *Econometrica* 64 (6): 1263–97.

Oulton, N. 2001. "Must the Growth Rate Decline? Baumol's Unbalanced Growth Revisited." *Oxford Economic Papers* 53 (4): 605–27.

Reimers, M., and S. Klasen. 2013. "Revisiting the Role of Education for Agricultural Productivity." *American Journal of Agricultural Economics* 95 (1): 131–52.

Schimmelpfennig, D., and C. Thirtle. 1999. "The Internationalization of Agricultural Technology: Patents, R&D Spillovers, and Their Effects on Productivity in the European

Union and United States." *Contemporary Economic Policy* 17 (4): 457–68.

Schumacher, E. F. 1973. *Small Is Beautiful: Economics as If People Mattered.* New York: Harper Collins.

Sen, A. K. 1966. "Peasants and Dualism with or without Surplus Labor." *Journal of Political Economy* 74 (5): 425–50.

Sinha, R. 2019a. "Distortions in Intermediate Markets and Structural Transformation in Latin America." Working paper, World Bank, Washington, DC.

Sinha, R. 2019b. "What Explains Latin America's Low Share of Industrial Employment?" Policy Research Working Paper 8791, World Bank, Washington, DC.

Solis, D., B. E. Bravo-Ureta, and R. E. Quiroga. 2009. "Technical Efficiency among Peasant Farmers Participating in Natural Resource Management Programmes in Central America." *Journal of Agricultural Economics* 60 (1): 202–19.

Stifel, D., and B. Minten. 2008. "Isolation and Agricultural Productivity." *Agricultural Economics* 39 (1): 1–15.

Thirtle, C., L. Lin, and J. Piesse. 2003. "The Impact of Research-Led Agricultural Productivity Growth on Poverty Reduction in Africa, Asia and Latin America." *World Development* 31 (12): 1959–75.

Timmer, M. P., G. J. de Vries, and K. de Vries. 2015. "Patterns of Structural Change in Developing Countries." In *Routledge Handbook of Industry and Development,* edited by J. Weiss and M. Tribe, 65–83. Abingdon-on-Thames, UK: Routledge.

Trindade, F. J., and L. E. Fulginiti. 2015. "Is There a Slowdown in Agricultural Productivity Growth in South America?" *Agricultural Economics* 46 (SI): 69–81.

Economic transformation, skills, and the future of work | 3

Chapter 2 described how technological changes, income effects, and consumer preferences are changing the structure of economies in the Latin America and the Caribbean (LAC) region. This chapter shifts attention to the impacts that this economic transformation and the emergence of new technologies will have on jobs, occupations, and the demand for skills.

Recently, much attention has been devoted to the potential impacts of emerging technologies. Under the banner of the Fourth Industrial Revolution are technological innovations such as artificial intelligence (AI), Internet of Things (IoT), and 3D printing. Meanwhile, a flurry of reports and books have appeared aimed at trying to understand the impact of these technologies on the labor market and the jobs of the future.[1]

Fears around the concept of "technological unemployment" have made headlines and dominate the concerns of policy makers and workers alike. Technological unemployment refers to the notion that technological innovations such as AI and automation will take over most of the production tasks in the economy, leaving humans without work. The fear of machines taking over jobs is not new and in fact has

been around for centuries. Perhaps most famously, in England in the early nineteenth century members of the Luddite movement sabotaged new textile machines to defend their jobs. And yet economic history has proven these concerns unfounded. Time and time again, technological innovations have spurred dramatic productivity gains that increased standards of living and created many more jobs than they destroyed.

As will be discussed shortly in more detail, the total impact of automation is hard to forecast because the effects of innovations tend to be widespread and ripple throughout the economy. In essence, new technologies that increase productivity have general equilibrium effects that increase the demand for labor across the economy. The simplistic idea that an economy has a fixed number of tasks is known as the "lump of labor fallacy." Innovations may generate jobs in the industry where they are applied, but also in industries that are connected (through either backward or forward linkages) to that industry and even in unrelated industries. History also teaches us that innovations can create jobs that do not even exist today.

As described in this chapter, however, the labor market is already changing. During the

1990s and the early 2000s, the main concern of labor economists was the rising wage inequality in both developed and developing economies. Over time, new evidence has emerged for advanced economies indicating that jobs and occupations in the middle of the wage distribution have been shrinking—a phenomenon dubbed labor market polarization. To explain this phenomenon, economists rely on a new theory known as routine-biased technological change (RBTC), which suggests that recent technological change is biased toward replacing labor in routine tasks.

Although there is mixed evidence that this polarization in the labor market has reached developing countries (Maloney and Molina 2016; Messina, Oveido, and Pica 2016), there is growing concern that it will reach these countries sooner rather than later. This is of special concern to economies in the LAC region, which are already exhibiting high levels of wage inequality.

This chapter begins by discussing the changes in the labor market already under way in the LAC region. Although there is little evidence of labor market polarization in the region, this study found substantial changes in the composition of occupations in the economy—in particular, a shift away from occupations that are intensive in routine manual (RM) tasks (such as machine operator and assembler) toward occupations that are intensive in nonroutine analytical or cognitive tasks (such as lawyer, scientist, and manager) and nonroutine interpersonal tasks (such as teacher, manager, and personal trainer).

It then discusses the effects of automation on jobs in general and presents estimates, using different methodologies, of the potential job losses in the LAC economies. It is important to note upfront that the estimated range of potential job losses is very wide, and it clearly reflects the limited understanding of this issue. Perhaps more important, these estimates are based on technological feasibility rather than economic incentives, and these methodologies are designed to capture only a measure of jobs at risk and not potential jobs created.

Finally, this chapter highlights the policies that governments must institute to guard against the potential adjustment costs brought about by technological innovations. As some occupations are replaced by machines, new ones will appear as well. Nevertheless, it is clear that workers will interact with more machines and will be expected to understand increasingly complex technologies. They therefore will need the capabilities and skills to adjust to these new demands.

Investing in the human capital of the workforce continues to be the best policy to insure against the risk of automation and should be a priority for policy makers. Although investing in early childhood education generates the highest return on investment (World Bank 2019), there is room to improve in every dimension of the educational system. In recent decades, many LAC countries have made substantial progress in improving access to secondary education, but the quality of education continues to lag that of advanced nations and developing country peers in East Asia.

What may become more important as new automation technologies are adopted in LAC countries is adult learning and retraining programs. Although the time frame for the adoption of technology is not clear, it is possible that transformations in the workplace will happen midcareer for many workers, and so they will need to adapt and adjust, particularly to the changing set of tasks they must perform at work. To minimize the adjustment costs borne by workers, governments should support programs that help workers upskill and retrain for these new jobs and tasks.

The labor market is already changing

From production to services

As argued in this report, potent economic forces are transforming the global economy, shifting employment away from production (agriculture and industry) and into the services sector. Two factors are at work.

First, as incomes rise, consumers tend to devote a larger share of their expenditures to services. Second, technological progress is more acute in the agriculture and industrial sectors, thereby pushing workers into the services sector.

Compounding this shift in the economic structure is a transformation of occupations within broad economic sectors. Duernecker and Herrendorf (2017) propose a new model of structural transformation that distinguishes between broad categories of occupations instead of broad categories of industries. They categorize occupations using the same underlying principle as for industries: goods occupations such as farm workers and machine operators produce tangible value added; service occupations such as clerks and managers produce intangible value added. With this novel classification and using 182 harmonized census data for 67 countries, Duernecker and Herrendorf (2017) show that as gross domestic product (GDP) per capita increases, employment in goods occupations decreases, whereas it increases in service occupations. More surprising, however, is that as GDP per capita increases, the employment share of service occupations increases in *all* economic sectors. Therefore, workers are shifting toward service occupations (producing intangible value added) in the services sector but also in the goods-producing sector. This result is intimately related to the "servicification" of manufacturing phenomenon described in chapter 2.

This study replicates the analysis by Duernecker and Herrendorf (2017) and finds that these shifts are present in LAC countries as well. As Latin American economies have grown over time, the share of workers employed in goods occupations has fallen, while the share in service occupations has risen (see figure 3.1, panels a and b). A more detailed analysis shows that the decline in goods occupations is related to declines in both the agriculture sector and the industrial sector. Perhaps related to the premature deindustrialization hypothesis, the graphs reveal that LAC countries appear to have fewer goods occupations and more service occupations than expected given the level of development.

Table 3.1 presents estimates on how the composition of occupations changes over the development process. Clearly, not only does economic development bring a shift in the total employment levels per sector, but also within sectors the input allocation of labor changes. In other words, as economies develop, each economic sector employs relatively fewer people directly in the production process and more people who are producing intangible value added.

Thus two effects are changing the nature of jobs in the same direction. First, technological innovations and rising incomes are pushing production and workers away from agriculture and manufacturing and toward the services sector. Second, compounding this effect is the change in the composition of occupations under way *within* each broad economic sector. In other words, within the manufacturing and agriculture sectors, occupations are shifting away from production toward service occupations (that is, more managers and professionals and fewer farm workers and machine operators). The picture that emerges is one in which the jobs of the future will be mostly service occupations that are increasingly concentrated in the services sector. Most important for policy makers, service occupations require skills very different from those needed for production-related occupations. The following section turns to this issue.

From skill-biased technological change to routine-biased technological change

Recent evidence in the academic literature points to a labor market that is changing rapidly and significantly. Starting from the observation that job loss and job creation patterns are not random, labor economists have developed different hypotheses to explain the observed patterns. What is clear is the significant shift in the demand for skills.

During the 1990s and early 2000s, wage inequality was rising in developed and

FIGURE 3.1   **Development of goods and service occupations, LAC and rest of world**

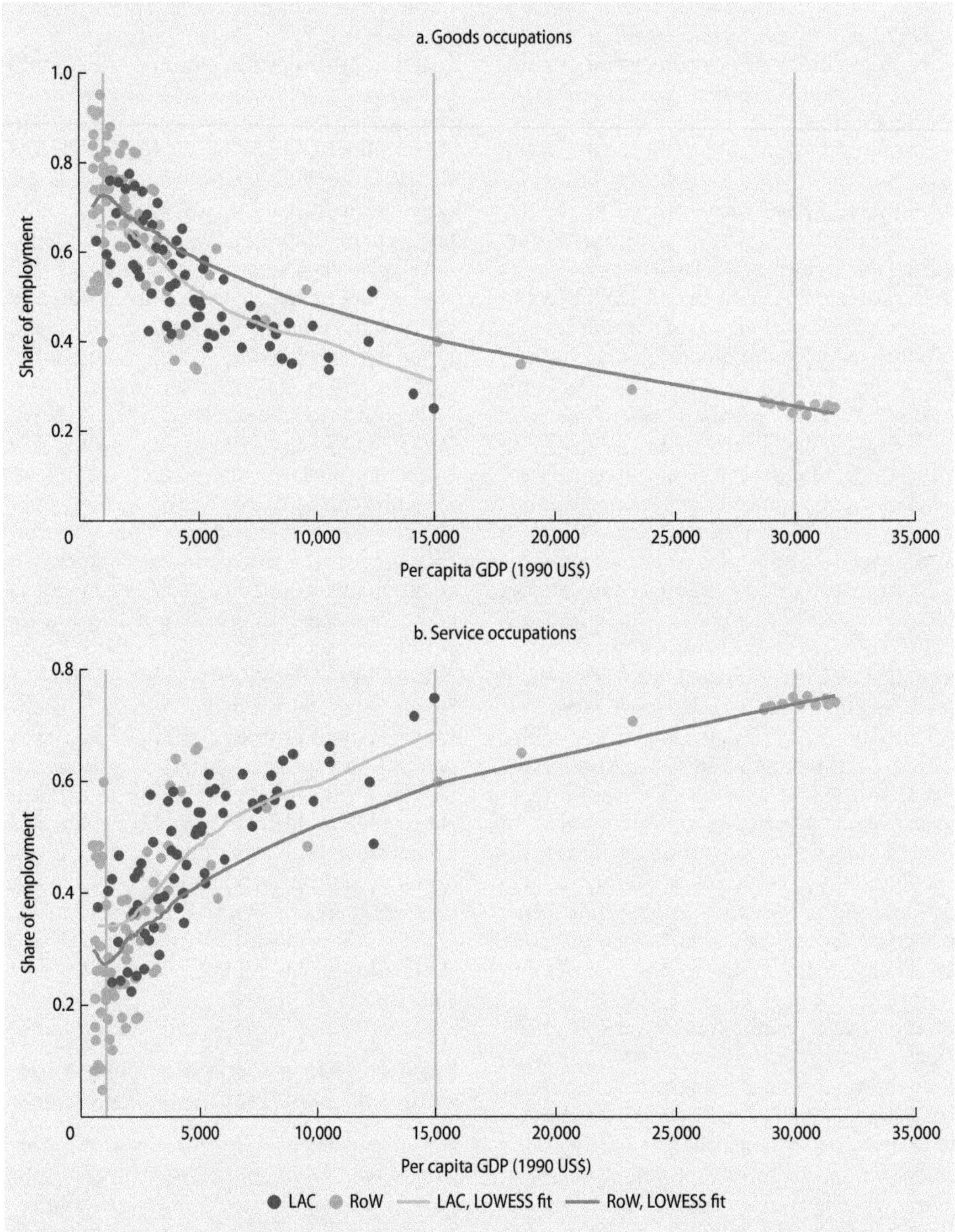

Sources: Original calculations for this publication using IPUMS International Database (Minnesota Population Center 2019); Maddison Database
(Bolt et al. 2018).
Note: Vertical green lines mark the values 1,000, 15,000, and 30,000 for which employment shares appear in table 3.1. GDP = gross domestic product
LAC = Latin America and the Caribbean; LOWESS = locally weighted polynomial regression; RoW = rest of world.

TABLE 3.1   **Reallocation of occupations within sectors over development process**

GDP per capita (1990 US$)	Goods sector			Services sector		
	1,000	**15,000**	**30,000**	**1,000**	**15,000**	**30,000**
Employment share (%) of						
Goods occupations	0.97	0.75	0.60	0.17	0.14	0.11
Service occupations	0.03	0.25	0.40	0.83	0.86	0.89

Source: Original calculations for this publication using IPUMS International Database (Minnesota Population Center 2019).
Note: Shares are calculated from fitted LOWESS curves. GDP = gross domestic product; LOWESS = locally weighted polynomial regression.

developing economies. In particular, it was documented that the skill premium (the extra income earned by educated workers) was rising. Labor economists hypothesized that technological innovations were benefiting educated workers more relative to less skilled workers. This so-called skill-biased technological change (SBTC) theory essentially explained the increase in the wage premium of educated workers by suggesting that new technologies were making highly skilled workers more productive. In other words, technological innovations were complementary to educated workers. As a result, they became more productive and more in demand, ultimately leading to higher wages for the skilled workforce. For a couple of decades, the theory and the empirical tests and evidence worked well in explaining the patterns observed in the data.

Over time, however, new evidence showed a hollowing out of jobs and occupations that were in the middle of the wage distribution in developed economies. Although jobs were still being created at both ends of the skill spectrum (low skilled and high skilled), the middle-skilled jobs were disappearing. This phenomenon is known as labor market polarization. Specifically, high-paying jobs such as managerial, professional, and associate professional occupations are experiencing rapid increases in their employment shares. In addition, the employment shares for low-paid service workers such as domestic helpers, cleaners, security personnel, and those in catering and personal care have increased. By contrast, the employment shares of middle-paying jobs such as office clerks, craft and related trades workers, and plant and machine operators and assemblers

have declined. This phenomenon has been well documented for the United States and the United Kingdom, Germany, and other major economies of Western Europe.[2]

To explain these new patterns in the labor market, economists developed a new theory, RBTC. Essentially, routine tasks are a limited and well-defined set of cognitive and manual activities that can be accomplished by following explicit rules. For example, picking, sorting, and repetitive assembly are RM tasks; record-keeping, calculation, and repetitive customer service (such as bank tellers) are examples of routine cognitive (RC) tasks. Nonroutine tasks are those that cannot be easily codified or defined in explicit rules. These tasks can be cognitive such as problem solving, complex communication activities, and forming and testing hypotheses. They can be manual as well—for example, driving and sports activities.

RBTC models generally posit that computers and robots are more substitutable for human labor in carrying out routine tasks than nonroutine tasks. Routine and nonroutine tasks are themselves imperfect substitutes, and a greater intensity of routine inputs increases the marginal product of nonroutine inputs. According to Autor and Dorn (2013, 1559), "The secularly falling price of accomplishing routine tasks using computer capital complements the 'abstract' creative, problem-solving, and coordination tasks performed by highly-educated workers such as professionals and managers, for whom data analysis is an input into production. Critically, automation of routine tasks neither directly substitutes for nor complements the core jobs tasks of low education occupations—service occupations in particular—that rely heavily on 'manual' tasks such as physical dexterity and flexible interpersonal communication. Consequently, as computerization erodes the wage paid to routine tasks in the model, low-skill workers reallocate their labor supply to service occupations."

This new theory seems to fit the experience of developed economies quite well. What has been the experience of developing countries? Is labor market polarization occurring there as well? Will the same patterns materialize? And where does the LAC region stand in this debate? This chapter turns to these questions next.

Labor market polarization in the developing world: Is it coming?

To date, there is mixed evidence of labor market polarization in developing countries. On the one hand, even if polarization has not yet occurred, it may be around the corner as technological innovations are dispersed and adopted around the developing world. On the other hand, there are many reasons why the experience of developing countries need not be the same as that of advanced economies.

Maloney and Molina (2016) offer several possible reasons why labor market polarization may never happen or may be more muted in some countries. First, initial occupation distributions may be very different in developing economies. For one thing, they may not have many workers engaged in the routine tasks commonly associated with manufacturing and routine clerical work in offices. This argument is particularly relevant for lower-income countries where industrialization may be limited (and routine manufacturing jobs are few) and where many workers are engaged in primary and elementary occupations. Thus few workers engaged largely in routine tasks would be displaced. In the context of the LAC region, this argument may be relevant to Bolivia, Haiti, and some Central American countries.

Second, jobs offshored from advanced economies may be filling in (as opposed to hollowing out) the middle-skilled jobs in developing economies. This could be particularly important for Mexico and some economies in Central America, which may receive the manufacturing jobs being offshored from the United States.

Third, new technologies may lower barriers to entry and facilitate information flows on markets and opportunities, potential products, inputs, and production technologies to enable the creation of new industries such as travel services, finance, tourism, and international marketing of local products. Meanwhile, the impact of technological innovations in developing countries is unclear. Some evidence suggests that adoption of information and communications technology (ICT) is strongly correlated with job polarization (Michaels, Natraj, and Van Reenen 2013). However, ICT-related capital stocks are lower in developing countries (Eden and Gaggl 2015), and so the displacement effects on jobs directly affected by ICT may be more muted.

As will be argued in more detail shortly, adoption of labor-saving technologies that increase productivity and lower final prices may result in higher employment levels if the demand for these products or services are elastic—meaning that an increase in quantity demanded will more than compensate for the fall in price. Another argument relates to the degree to which automation is adopted because it depends on several factors: skill of the workforce, maintenance capacity, and technological absorptive capacity, among others. Adoption of automation technologies may therefore take a long time, depending on these initial conditions. Meanwhile, polarization implies higher employment in the types of occupations that complement automation. If a country does not have a broad, highly skilled workforce, then this employment growth would never occur, limiting labor force polarization.

Labor market polarization in the developing world: The evidence

The different sources of data on employment, tasks, and occupations have produced mixed findings on labor market polarization. Based on harmonized labor surveys and Autor's (2014) classification, the

World Development Report 2016: Digital Dividends (World Bank 2016, 120) states that

> ... there are signs that employment is also polarizing in a number of low- and middle-income countries. The average decline in the share of routine employment has been 0.39 percentage points a year, or 7.8 percentage points for the period. China is an exception, since the mechanization of agriculture increased the share of routine employment. Labor markets in low-income countries such as Ethiopia, with a large share of employment in manual occupations, are also not polarizing; neither is employment in Mongolia or Latin American countries where other factors—such as a commodity-driven boom benefiting low-skilled workers—could play a larger role in shaping labor markets.

On the other hand, Maloney and Molina (2016), using harmonized census data, do not find strong evidence of polarization in developing economies. They find that the key occupational categories associated with routine tasks are not decreasing, even in relative terms, for most countries in the sample. However, they do find relative declines in these types of occupations in Brazil, Indonesia, and Mexico, which could suggest potential polarizing forces.

Both results are based on analyzing the changes in occupational structure within countries over time. Following Autor (2014), occupations are classified as low, medium, or high skilled. Specifically, medium-skilled occupations are white-collar clerical, administrative, and sales occupations, as well as blue-collar production, craft, and operative occupations. Therefore, using either harmonized census data or harmonized labor surveys, the analysis focuses on the relative growth of each occupational category.

What is missing from this analysis is the fact that the set of tasks within an occupation is not fixed over time. Thus the demand for skills may be changing even if the occupational structure is not changing significantly. In fact, Autor, Levy, and Murnane (2003) and Spitz-Oener (2006) find that in

response to the introduction of automation technologies, workers adjusted their work time toward tasks complementary to the ones performed by machines. Moreover, analysis of worker-level information on the tasks performed in an occupation reveals that workers' task structures differ remarkably within occupations (Autor and Handel 2013). Cross-country differences are relevant as well. Messina, Oviedo, and Pica (2016) conclude: "Comparing task intensity scores in those countries and the U.S. shows that while the abstract content of jobs is similar in North- and South-America, the routine and manual contents are different. We speculate that the reason may be that Latin American occupations comprise a more heterogeneous set of tasks." Therefore, it is important to consider not only the evolution of the occupational structure, but also how the task content of occupations is changing over time.

The changing demand for skills in the LAC region

What follows is a description of the results of this study's analysis of the evolution of the demand for human skills for 11 LAC countries from 2000 to 2014. The study follows the methodology proposed by Autor, Levy, and Murnane (2003) and updated by Acemoglu and Autor (2011). The approach conceptualizes and measures skills by assessing the specific tasks associated with different occupations rather than measuring the educational credentials of workers performing those tasks. As is standard in the literature, five skills are assessed: routine manual (RM), nonroutine manual physical (NR-MP), routine cognitive (RC), nonroutine cognitive analytical (NR-CA), and nonroutine cognitive interpersonal (NR-CP).

The analysis relies on the ex post harmonized household surveys for each country-year prepared by the World Bank and the Center for Distributive, Labor and Social Studies at the Universidad de la Plata in Argentina (SEDLAC). These labor and household income surveys are generally nationally representative, and they provide information on the size of the household, demographics, and educational attainment, and, more important, detailed information on employment. The original (nonharmonized) country-specific occupational classifications are reclassified into the International Standard Classification of Occupations, version 1988 (ISCO-88), developed by the International Labour Organization. All occupations contained in the household surveys are then matched with their respective skill content from the US Department of Labor's Occupational Information Network (O*NET) database (https://www.onetonline.org/).

An important caveat for this analysis is that O*NET is taken as the primary reference because there are no country-year specific catalogs of skill content for LAC countries.[3] Essentially, it is assumed that the skill content of a given occupation is comparable internationally. The validity of this assumption may differ across certain occupations or country contexts. As noted by Aedo et al. (2013, 9), "countries differ in technology and regulatory contexts which may employ different skill

profiles for specific occupations. For example, teachers in low-income settings are more likely to lack the tools (especially ICT tools) that support innovative teaching than teachers in developed countries. Similarly, doctors or nurses might have access to equipment as well as medical knowledge which impacts the skill content and mix they can bring to bear in different settings." The authors then postulate that occupations intensive in nonroutine tasks are probably more skill-intensive in more advanced economic settings than in lower-income ones. If true, this would suggest a potential upward bias in the measured skill intensity of nonroutine (both analytical and interpersonal) skills.[4]

Measurement of task content is usually based on data that stem from either the expert-based approach or the worker-based approach. Box 3.1 describes these approaches and their pros and cons.

Anyone interpreting the results of this analysis should note that the values of the indexes are not strictly comparable across countries.

BOX 3.1   **What are workers doing?**

Jobs in an economy are indexed to a set of occupations that develop tasks. These tasks have been categorized in the literature as routinary or nonroutinary—see Acemoglu and Autor (2011) and Autor, Levy, and Murnane (2003). The first category consists of manual and specific activities generally more prone to automation and replicability by machines or computers. The second category is composed of more complex activities in which abstraction and socioemotional skills play an important role. Measuring task content, however, is not straightforward, and the two main streams of data that inform research are provided either by a pool of experts on a fixed number of occupations (expert-based approach) or by workers who identify their task content relying on their own experience (worker-based approach).

Expert-based approach

This approach hinges on the fact that a group of respondents—job incumbents, occupation experts,

and industrial psychologists—are interviewed to weigh in on the importance of a given occupation by scoring the importance or intensity of different tasks in the workplace. A common source of information is the Occupational Information Network (O*NET),[a] which covers nearly 1,000 occupations in the United States. At the outset, O*NET operates by providing information on work-oriented descriptors (such as worker characteristics, worker requirements, and experience requirements) and job-oriented descriptors (such as occupational requirements, workforce characteristics, and occupation-specific information) that account for tasks. These assessments are updated periodically to reflect changes in the occupational structure of the US economy, using as point of reference the Standard Occupational Classification (SOC).

The expert-based approach has been widely used in studies aimed at understanding occupation dynamics (for example, Acemoglu and Autor 2011; Autor

Box continues next page

What are workers doing? *(continued)*

and Dorn 2009; Goos and Manning 2007; Goos, Manning, and Salomons 2009). One advantage of this approach is that it serves as a rich source of information on tasks over time that can also be extrapolated to other economies. However, such transition through reference crosswalks has been criticized for the glaring bias produced by assuming that the task content is the same as in the United States, mainly from O*NET data.[b]

Worker-based approach

Unlike the expert-based approach, this way of measuring tasks is taken from workers using specific surveys. Workers are interviewed and asked about their cognitive and noncognitive traits at work. Two common sources of information are the World Bank's STEP (Skills Toward Employability and Productivity) Skills Measurement Program for developing countries and the Programme for the International Assessment of Adult Competencies (PIAAC) for Organisation for Economic Co-operation and Development (OECD) countries.[c] STEP and PIAAC ask random individuals, ages 15–65, about their household characteristics in the areas of health, education, training, and employment. Moreover, data are collected on cognitive and socioemotional skills that reflect the complexity and frequency of reading, writing,

and math use; physical (manual) requirements; and interpersonal activities at work.

The main advantage of using the worker-based approach is that it avoids the problems of measurement error when ascribing data from the United States[d] (via O*NET) to, for example, developing economies. Nevertheless, the response bias produced by the large variance in the computation of task indicators within occupations could be problematic. The underrepresentation of occupations because of small samples that do not cover all economic sectors could also hinder comparability vis-à-vis studies based on the expert-based approach.

a. Another reference for the United States is the *Dictionary of Occupational Titles* (DOT), a previous version of O*NET also sponsored by the US Department of Labor but currently outdated in the literature.
b. See, for example, Hardy, Keister, and Lewandowski (2018) for an application in Eastern Europe and Aedo et al. (2013) for a cross-country comparison using household surveys and O*NET.
c. https://microdata.worldbank.org/index.php/catalog /step/about); https://www.oecd.org/skills/piaac/.
d. Dicarlo et al. (2016) find that data on nonroutine tasks in developing countries are more likely to resemble data from the United States. A low correlation is reported for routine tasks, meaning that expert-based approaches overestimate the task content of basic repetitive tasks.

Thus a higher value of the index of NR-CA skills at the endpoint does not imply that more of those skills are found in one country than another. Instead, it implies that the country has changed its occupational structure in favor of those skills at a higher rate. Therefore, it is possible to compare the rate of change (trends) across countries over time.

The general results are for the most part consistent with the findings of the literature in both developed and developing countries. Figure 3.2, panels a and b, reveal that most countries in the LAC region have experienced increases in the analytical (panel a) and interpersonal (panel b) tasks within the nonroutine cognitive task component. In the case of NR-CA tasks, Costa Rica has grown the most, followed by Ecuador, Nicaragua, Peru, and Colombia.

Uruguay, Brazil, and Chile show a slower but still important growth rate in the usage of these skills, whereas the Dominican Republic and El Salvador exhibit slow growth rates. Mexico exhibits a decrease in the use of NR-CA tasks, a surprising result that may stem in part from certain data restrictions. Because Mexico changed its occupational classification in 2008, the analysis was restricted to the 2000–2008 timeframe. The year 2008 was marked by the beginning of the global financial crisis, which also may have affected the results.

For NR-CP skills the story is similar. A first group of countries composed of Costa Rica, Ecuador, and Nicaragua lead the pack with very strong growth rates, while a second group, comprising the Dominican Republic, Uruguay, El Salvador, and Peru, also show

FIGURE 3.2   Evolution of task content of jobs (mean change): 11 LAC countries, 2000–2014

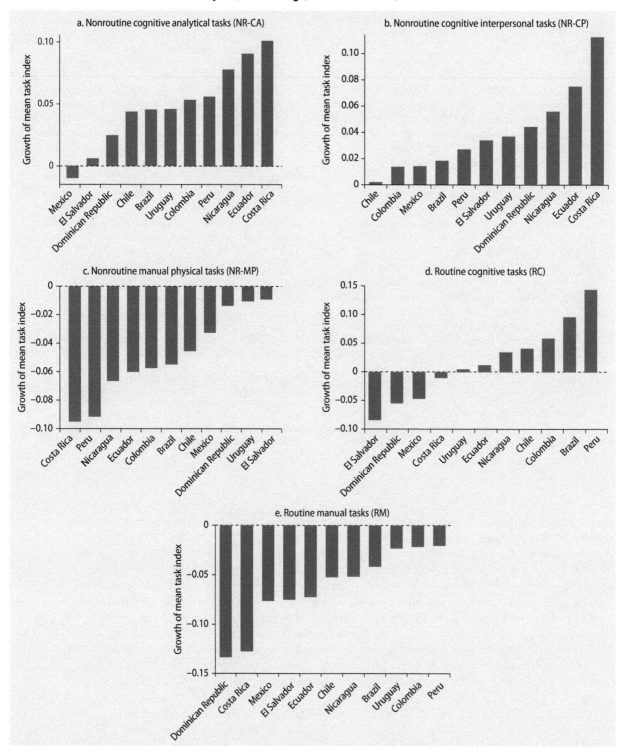

Source: Original calculations for this publication using Socio-Economic Database for Latin America and the Caribbean (SEDLAC) household surveys, CEDLAS and World Bank (https://datacatalog.worldbank.org/dataset/socio-economic-database-latin-america-and-caribbean).
Note: CEDLAS = Center for Distributive, Labor and Social Studies; LAC = Latin America and the Caribbean.

strong growth rates. Behind are Brazil, Mexico, Colombia, and Chile with smaller increases.

The time trends for NR-MP in panel c are consistent with the findings of previous studies. Throughout the region, there is a marked trend of declining NR-MP tasks. The largest declines are observed for Costa Rica and Peru, followed by Nicaragua and Ecuador. Panel e paints a similar picture for RM tasks. The Dominican Republic and Costa Rica show the largest declines. Essentially, all countries in the region are experiencing a shift away from NR-MP and RM, albeit at different paces.

The findings on RC tasks are mixed (figure 3.2, panel d). They have increased in many countries of the region (strongly in Peru and Brazil), while declining in others, most noticeably in El Salvador. A similar result is reported by Hardy, Keister, and Lewandowski (2016) for a sample of 10 Eastern European countries.[5] The authors attribute the different findings across countries to a combination of varying rates of structural changes and shifts toward work with a lower speed of deroutinization. This result contrasts with the experience of developed countries, where there is a clear and marked decline of occupations with RC-intensive tasks. This finding should be of concern to policy makers in the region. The evidence in advanced nations suggests that the technologies that could replace these types of tasks already exist and could be adopted in the LAC region in the near future. Thus these occupations may be at risk of changing or disappearing in the next decade or so, depending on the rate of technology adoption.

What follows is a description of the results that emerge from a timeline analysis of the two major economic sectors (industrial and services) for 11 countries in the LAC region.[6] Following the same standardization procedures as earlier, the evolution of the task component indexes for the sample of workers employed in each sector is described separately. Thus the results presented speak only to the changes in task utilization within each sector and abstracts from the effects of reallocation of labor across sectors.

Industrial sector

Figure 3.3, panels a and b, describes the evolution of NR-CA and NR-CP in the industrial sector (mining and quarrying, manufacturing, construction, and utilities). Both graphs tell the same story: an increase in the intensity of both NR-CA and NR-CP in the industrial sector. Among these, two groups emerge. Nicaragua, Peru, El Salvador, the Dominican Republic, Ecuador, Costa Rica, and Brazil show the highest rates of transition toward NR-CA– and NR-CP–intensive occupations. Following at a more modest pace are Chile, Colombia, Mexico, and Uruguay.

Panel c of figure 3.3 shows that in the industrial sector NR-MP labor tasks have increased across all countries. The changes are most profound in Chile, Ecuador, El Salvador, and Brazil, and are more moderate in Costa Rica, Nicaragua, Colombia, and the Dominican Republic. Panels d and e of figure 3.3 describe the evolution of RC tasks and RM tasks in the industrial sector. The results closely mirror those for nonroutine tasks. In most countries, they decrease.

These results suggest that production processes within the industrial sector of the region are changing, adopting more nonroutine cognitive and manual tasks. At the same time, and consistent with the literature on automation and robotization, the demand for skills in the region is moving away from routine tasks, both cognitive and manual.

At this point a cautionary note is warranted. As noted earlier, this analysis is based on the O*NET classification of tasks in both the base year of 2003 and the updated version of 2017. Use of both catalogs allows incorporation into the analysis the possible changes in tasks within occupations over time. In other words, workers in the same occupation may be performing a different set of tasks between the two points in time. Adoption of new technologies, for example, may replace part of the tasks performed in an occupation, thereby allowing the workers to spend more time on other tasks and changing the task intensity within an occupation. Thus the assumption in this analysis is that the changes in tasks in the United States have

FIGURE 3.3   **Evolution of task content of jobs in industrial sector: 11 LAC countries, 2000–2014**

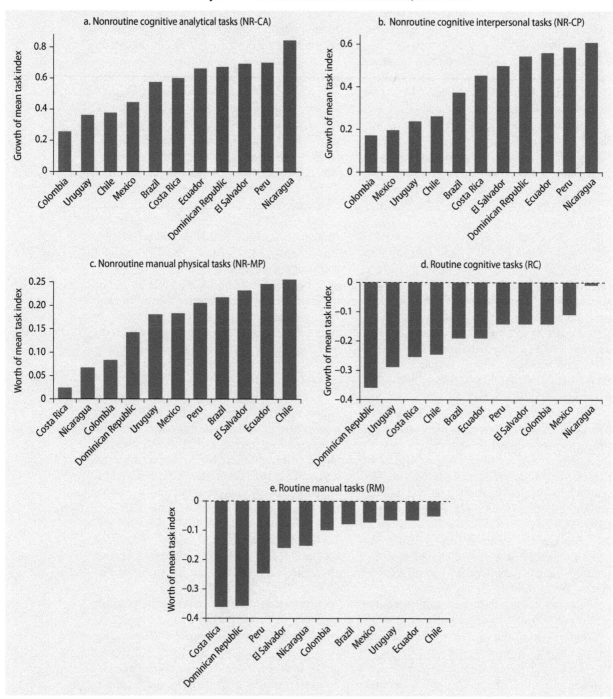

Source: Original calculations for this publication using Socio-Economic Database for Latin America and the Caribbean (SEDLAC) household surveys, CEDLAS and World Bank (https:// datacatalog.worldbank.org/dataset/socio-economic-database-latin-america-and-caribbean).
Note: CEDLAS = Center for Distributive, Labor and Social Studies; LAC = Latin America and the Caribbean.

occurred in LAC countries as well and to the same extent.

What follows is a simple decomposition of the overall results for the industrial sector into three components: (1) between occupations (changes in the occupational structure within the industrial sector), (2) within occupations (how tasks have changed in that occupation), and (3) the interaction between these two. This decomposition allows disentanglement of some heterogeneous patterns that are observed across countries.

Figure 3.4 presents the results of this simple decomposition for NR-CA tasks (panel a)

FIGURE 3.4 Decomposition of task content in industrial sector: 11 LAC countries, 2000–2014

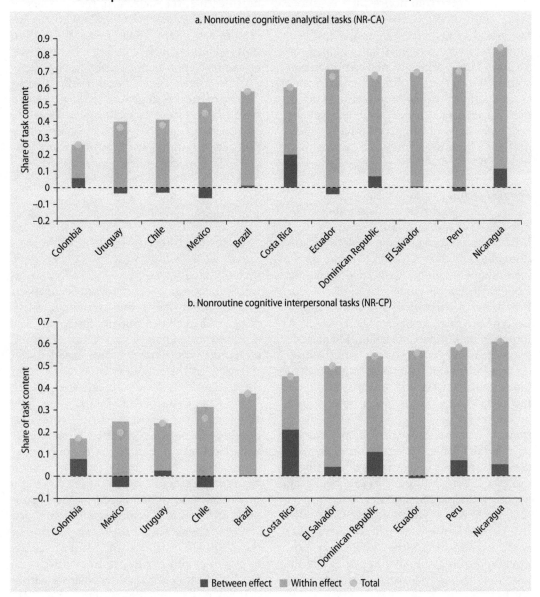

Source: Original calculations for this publication using Socio-Economic Database for Latin America and the Caribbean (SEDLAC) household surveys, CEDLAS and World Bank (https://datacatalog.worldbank.org/dataset/socio-economic-database-latin-america-and-caribbean).
Note: Figure shows decomposition of the overall results for the industrial sector into three components: (1) between occupations (changes in the occupational structure within the industrial sector); (2) within occupations (how tasks have changed in that occupation); and (3) the interaction between these two. CEDLAS = Center for Distributive, Labor and Social Studies; LAC = Latin America and the Caribbean.

and NR-CP tasks (panel b). The patterns just described are for the most part the result of within-occupation changes. Interestingly, in five countries—Chile, Ecuador, Mexico, Peru, and Uruguay—the changes between occupations contributed negatively to the overall nonroutine cognitive results. In other words, over time the industrial sector in these economies has changed its occupational structure away from nonroutine cognitive tasks. This effect is completely reversed, however, by the increase in nonroutine cognitive tasks within occupations. Thus if one assumes that workers in the LAC region in a specific occupation did not change their tasks at all (no within-occupation changes), then the industrial sector in Chile, Ecuador, Peru, Mexico, and Uruguay would have seen declines in the use of nonroutine cognitive tasks.

Services sector

Figure 3.5 reveals that in the services sector NR-CP tasks (panel b) are increasing in all LAC countries except Chile, Colombia, and Uruguay, and NR-CA tasks (panel a) are increasing strongly in Peru, Nicaragua, and Ecuador, increasing moderately in El Salvador, Brazil, and Costa Rica, and decreasing in Colombia, Chile, Uruguay, the Dominican Republic, and Mexico. Ecuador, El Salvador, Nicaragua, and Peru stand out with the highest growth rates in both tasks. Panels c and e indicate that the services sector is also moving away from manual tasks, both routine and nonroutine. Finally, panel d also reflects important increases in the intensity of RC tasks for all LAC countries. The increase in the use of RC tasks is somewhat at odds with the results for developed countries and the RBTC hypothesis. In fact, Autor, Levy, and Murnane (2003) and Acemoglu and Autor (2011) find that occupations intensive in RC tasks (such as clerical and administrative) are among the group of occupations that are declining the most in the United States, and a similar result has been found for Western European countries (Goos et al. 2014).

Thus it appears that the services sector in the LAC region is undergoing an important

transformation in its production process in which manual tasks are being replaced by more cognitive tasks (both routine and nonroutine). Starkest are the patterns of decreasing manual tasks, as economies move toward RC and NR-CP tasks, perhaps reflecting increases in more administrative or clerical work, as well as tasks that involve more teamwork or interactions with clients. As noted earlier, the increase in the intensity of RC skills is somewhat at odds with the literature for developed countries and should be a red flag for policy makers. The technology to replace workers in these types of tasks already exists, as evidenced by the relative decline of these occupations in the developed world. Therefore, as technology disperses and reaches LAC economies, it is very likely that workers in these types of occupations will face competition from machines and are perhaps at risk of losing their jobs.

Conclusions

In general, countries in the LAC region appear to be shifting away from occupations that are intensive in manual tasks (both routine and nonroutine) and toward occupations that are intensive in nonroutine cognitive tasks (both analytical and interpersonal). The economywide changes in the occupational structure and therefore in the embedded skill intensity of the economy may result from three related but distinct economic forces.

First, as described in detail in the first chapter of this report, as LAC economies develop they are reallocating labor across broad economic sectors. Although some occupations appear in all sectors, in general structural transformation implies changes in the occupational structure of an economy. In fact, LAC countries experienced substantial structural transformation during the 2000–2014 time frame. In particular, as documented earlier, most countries in the LAC region are experiencing premature deindustrialization, which implies there are relatively fewer jobs in the industrial sector, whereas employment in the services sector has increased dramatically.

FIGURE 3.5 **Evolution of task content of jobs in services sector: 11 LAC countries, 2000–2014**

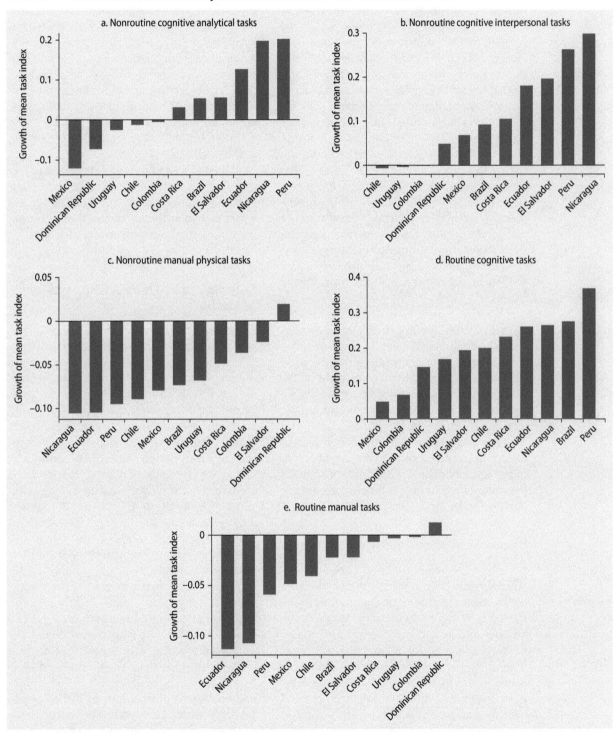

Source: Original calculations for this publication using Socio-Economic Database for Latin America and the Caribbean (SEDLAC) household surveys, CEDLAS and World Bank (https://datacatalog.worldbank.org/dataset/socio-economic-database-latin-america-and-caribbean).
Note: CEDLAS = Center for Distributive, Labor and Social Studies; LAC = Latin America and the Caribbean.

The second force is related to the technological progress that is changing the nature of production processes within all sectors of the economy. Duernecker and Herrendorf (2017) report that service occupation employment (such as managers and clerks) grows within the goods-producing sector (agriculture and industry in this study's classification) as GDP per capita increases. This is related as well to the phenomenon of servicification of manufacturing described in chapter 2. During this study's period of analysis, the LAC countries experienced sustained high growth rates, with higher GDP per capita at the end of the period. Because service occupations differ from goods occupations in skill intensities, a changing skill intensity usage within broad economic sectors should be expected as well.

Third, the adoption of technology in the workplace changes the set of tasks that workers perform as part of their occupation. Because automation and robotization take over the simpler, more routine tasks, workers have adapted by shifting their work time toward the more complex and harder to automate tasks. In fact, Autor, Levy, and Murnane (2003) and Spitz-Oener (2006) found that as a response to the introduction of automation technologies, workers adjusted their work time toward tasks complementary to those of the machines.

Looking into the future: Automation, tasks, and skills

Since the seminal paper by Frey and Osborne (2017) claiming that 47 percent of jobs in the United States were at risk of disappearing to automation, a flurry of reports and books have stoked fears of mass "technological unemployment." This concern is not new; it dates back to the beginning of the First Industrial Revolution and has been revived over time as powerful technological innovations have revolutionized the way goods and services are produced in an economy.

This section begins by organizing the general ideas about the impact of automation on jobs. What are the concerns expressed by techno-pessimists, who claim that the new technologies of the Fourth Industrial Revolution (such as artificial intelligence, machine learning, Internet of Things, additive manufacturing, and 3D printing) are different from any previous technological innovations? What are all the possible general equilibrium impacts of introducing new technologies into an economy? Which effect will be most important?

It then turns to how to measure the potential impact of automation on the total number of jobs, followed by estimates of job losses due to automation based on different methodologies and data sources for 16 LAC countries.

Automation and jobs: A history of fear of machines

Concerns about mass technological unemployment have been around for centuries. When clergyman William Lee applied for a royal patent for a knitting machine in 1589, Queen Elizabeth I of England pointed out, "Consider thou what the invention would do to my poor subjects. It would assuredly bring them to ruin by depriving them of employment" (McKinley 1958). Similarly, the Qing dynasty of China resisted the construction of railways because it was concerned about the potential impact on the luggage-carrying jobs (Zeng 1973). Perhaps most famously, the Luddite movement sabotaged new textile machines to defend their jobs in England.

And yet economic history has proven these concerns unfounded. Time and time again, technological innovations have spurred dramatic gains in productivity that have increased standards of living and created many more jobs than they destroyed. It is true that some jobs disappeared—machines replaced many skilled and unskilled workers over time. However, new jobs, some related to the new technologies and many not related, have been created over time. As a result, today a higher proportion of a much larger population is working. Thus the lesson

ECONOMIC TRANSFORMATION, SKILLS, AND THE FUTURE OF WORK

from history is that technological innovations have always created more jobs than they have destroyed.

Modern techno-pessimists are aware of the lessons from history, but they claim it is different this time. In general, those who fear a jobless future point to the increasingly rapid technological advances driven by digitization (and thus the availability of big data) and the exponential nature of computing power.[7] At first, advances in automation were limited to routine, repetitive tasks that followed regular rules that could be codified (Autor, Levy, and Murnane 2003). As discussed earlier, this explains the relative decrease in jobs intensive in RM tasks (mostly in manufacturing) and RC tasks (for example, clerks and bookkeepers). However, recent advances in robotics and AI are threatening to go beyond routine tasks, encroaching on a set of tasks that was thought to be the exclusive domain of humans. In 2003, Autor, Levy, and Murnane surmised that driving jobs were relatively safe from automation because driving required far too complex data processing, physical dexterity, situational awareness, and improvisation. Today, autonomous self-driving cars have logged thousands of miles on highways and city streets with huge success. Meanwhile, IBM's Watson has beat the champion on *Jeopardy!* and can identify cancers with more accuracy than humans (Brynjolfsson and McAfee 2014). Machines are successfully performing legal searches and writing small journalistic articles. Techno-pessimists thus argue that this new wave of technological innovation is encroaching on a whole new set of tasks: nonroutine tasks, both cognitive and manual. Therefore, machines could eventually (the time frame is not clear) replace humans in many if not all tasks in the economy.

Automation and jobs: General equilibrium effects

Perhaps the best way to understand the full impacts of the introduction of new technologies is to consider the three questions that

Daniel and Richard Susskind (2015) posit in their book about the future of professions:

1. What is the new quantity of tasks that must be carried out?
2. What is the nature of these tasks?
3. Who has the advantage in carrying out these tasks?

The first question refers to considering all the effects produced by introducing a new labor-saving technology into the economy. Although at first glance it may appear that these technologies can only destroy jobs by replacing humans, careful consideration of general equilibrium effects may indicate otherwise. The simplistic view is that machines replace only workers who perform tasks. It is based on the idea that there is a fixed number of tasks in an economy—the so-called lump of labor fallacy—and as machines perform more and more of these tasks, it comes at the expense of human workers for whom there will be fewer tasks to do. History, however, has taught a very powerful lesson: the number of tasks in an economy is not fixed, and in fact the total number of tasks has increased over time. Why? Several effects must be considered.

If a firm introduces a new technology that replaces workers, generally the productivity of that firm will rise. In competitive markets, this higher productivity would result in lower marginal costs and therefore falling prices. In turn, lower prices imply a higher demand for that product or service. How much the demand increases depends on the specific price elasticity of that product or service.[8] If the demand for a specific product is elastic, it may lead to an increase in the level of production (that is, the number of tasks to be performed) and thus could lead to more jobs being created in that firm or industry (see box 3.2 for some examples).

Another important effect to consider is that the increase in productivity and the potential increase in production resulting from higher demand in the original industry raises the demand for all industries connected to the original, both upstream and downstream. Thus new tasks will be created in industries

---

BOX 3.2   **When automation creates jobs**

History has witnessed several examples of technological innovations that automated production tasks in an industry and led to higher employment in that same industry. During the Industrial Revolution, the introduction of new machinery in the textile industry lead to the automation of about 98 percent of the labor required to weave a yard of cloth. However, the number of weaving jobs actually increased (Bessen 2016). Meanwhile, the productivity gains were so significant that they drove the price of cloth down significantly. Coupled with the highly elastic demand for clothes, it resulted in net job growth in the textile industry, despite the automation of most production tasks.

A similar story can be told about bank tellers after the introduction of automated teller machines (ATMs) in the United States. The ATM performed many of the tasks performed by bank tellers such as cash handling and simpler bank operations. As detailed in the case study of Bessen (2016), "the number

of fulltime equivalent bank tellers has grown since ATMs were widely deployed during the late 1990s and early 2000s. Indeed, since 2000, the number of fulltime equivalent bank tellers has increased 2.0% per annum, substantially faster than the entire labor force. Why didn't employment fall? Because the ATM allowed banks to operate branch offices at lower cost; this prompted them to open many more branches (their demand was elastic), offsetting the erstwhile loss in teller jobs."

There are other examples as well. The number of cashiers in retail has increased since barcode scanners were widely deployed during the 1980s, even though the scanners reduced cashiers' checkout times by 18–19 percent (Basker 2015). Electronic document discovery software for legal proceedings clearly replaces the work of paralegals, and yet even as it has grown into a billion-dollar industry the number of paralegals has grown robustly.

---

that supply the original industry, as well as industries that may use the products or services as inputs for their own production. One example could be the transport and logistics industries, which would see more demand for their services (more tasks to be performed) because of the increased production in the original industry.

The potential effects are not even confined to the industry where the innovation was introduced. The increase in productivity resulting from the adoption of new technology would lead to rises in income in the economy. These rises could lead in turn to an increase in the demand for goods and services that are completely unrelated to the original industry. For example, throughout history increases in the productivity of agriculture and manufacturing have led to a higher demand for hospitality services such as restaurants and hotels as well as leisure and entertainment activities. Therefore, an

increase in productivity in one industry can lead to the creation of new tasks in a completely different area of the economy.

Finally, the emergence of new technologies, particularly general-purpose ones,[9] tends to create new jobs and tasks that do not even exist today. In the early 1900s, 41 percent of the US workforce worked in agriculture. One hundred years later (and several innovations later), employment in agriculture is less than 2 percent, and employment in health care, finance, leisure, and entertainment (much of it in occupations that did not exist 100 years ago) far outweighs the number of workers in agriculture (Autor 2015). A more current example is the internet. This innovation has not only revolutionized access to information, but also created entirely new industries and jobs that did not exist 30 years ago such as search engine optimizers[10] or social media managers. By definition, these effects are hard to measure and foresee, but history teaches that new technologies generally lead to new occupations and tasks that cannot even be imagined today.

One important point relevant to developing nations is that automation in developed nations may have indirect effects—that is, firms in developed nations adopt automation technologies that allow them to *reshore* (the opposite of offshoring) production. Thus developing nations may suffer job losses, or jobs may never emerge in the economy because advanced nations are reshoring production by adopting labor-saving technologies.

Although the evidence on this point is scarce, Artuc, Christiaensen, and Winkler (2019) have investigated the labor market impacts in Mexico of exposure to US automation. They find that the ratio of employment in the tradable sector to population is not affected by exposure to US automation or by the decline in exports caused by US automation. However, the average effect hides differential effects observed in different local labor markets. On the one hand, areas that initially had a relatively higher share of manufacturing jobs susceptible to being replaced by automation did experience a decline in the ratio of manufacturing employment to population. On the other hand, areas in which the fraction of jobs susceptible to being automated was low experienced an increase in the manufacturing employment to population ratio.

Automation and jobs: Humans working against machines or humans working with machines?

The previous section established that the number of tasks in an economy is not fixed and the adoption of new technologies can in fact lead to more tasks being created. However, assessing whether this implies more employment opportunities for humans requires turning to questions 2 and 3 stated earlier:

2. What is the nature of these tasks?
3. Who has the advantage in carrying out these tasks (humans or machines)?

It is important to consider not only the total number of tasks created, but also whether these tasks are ones that humans have the advantage in performing (thereby creating more employment) or whether these tasks can also be best performed by machines (thereby not creating more employment for humans).

A simple example illustrates this point more clearly. In an industry in which workers perform two tasks, A and B, a new technology is introduced that can fully automate task A. The increased productivity resulting from adoption of automation technology leads to a drop in the price of the good (or service) produced, and demand is elastic so that demand for the good increases overall. This increase will lead in turn to an increase in the number of B tasks used as inputs. To the extent that B tasks are those in which humans have a relative comparative advantage, this advantage could lead to more tasks being performed by humans. However, if the B task is also susceptible to automation, then even if the demand for such tasks increases it will not lead to more employment for humans.

Thus to understand the total impact of automation on employment it is important to consider all three questions together. Not only is it important to consider all the possible general equilibrium effects that can result in more tasks being created in an economy, but it is equally important to assess whether the new tasks being created are those in which humans have an advantage in performing them or whether machines can also replace workers in performing them. As detailed in the models explaining labor market polarization, the introduction of technologies that automate certain tasks—principally the routine tasks of production—raises the value of complementary tasks—generally nonroutine tasks. As long as humans retain the comparative advantage in performing these complementary tasks, then automation can lead to new jobs, raising the total employment level.

It is important to note here that jobs and occupations generally do not consist of a single task. Instead, workers perform a whole set of tasks—a bundle of tasks—and thus machines do not generally replace a whole job or occupation but rather a subset of tasks, allowing workers to perform other sets of tasks. The next section returns to this point in more detail, discussing the susceptibility of jobs to automation and how the risk of automation is measured in the literature.

Finally, although the final result may be an economy that ends up with more tasks to be performed and many of these new tasks will be performed by humans, there are likely to be significant adjustment costs. As machines become more powerful, dexterous, and capable, the subset of tasks in which humans retain an advantage may shrink over time. The evidence indicates that these tasks will require more cognitive, analytical, creative, and interpersonal skills. Therefore, policy makers need to consider the urgency of instilling in the workforce of the future these higher-order skills. The policy implications are discussed at the end of this chapter, but first the next section looks at how the academic literature has taken on the challenge of measuring how many jobs are at risk of disappearing because of automation.

Measuring the risk of automation: Occupation-based versus task-based approach

Although fears of mass technological unemployment are not new and actually date back centuries, new fears were stoked by the research of Frey and Osborne (2017). In their paper, they claimed that up to 47 percent of jobs in the United States were at risk of being automated. Since then, a flurry of reports using different approaches and data have produced a wide range of estimates. But why do these estimates differ so much?

Essentially, there are two broad approaches to measuring the risk of automation of occupations. The first, the occupation-based approach, was developed by Frey and Osborne (2017). Subsequent research has criticized their approach, recognizing that occupations do not consist of a single task but rather a bundle of tasks. Therefore, although a subset of tasks within an occupation may be automated, that does not imply that the whole occupation will be automated or that the job will disappear entirely. The second approach, developed by Arntz, Gregory, and Zierahn (2016) and called the task-based approach, has produced estimates of the risks of automation that are significantly lower (9 percent for the United States). This section briefly describes each approach.

Occupation-based approach

Frey and Osborne (2017) based their analysis on the 2010 version of the O*NET database (box 3.1). This database describes the task content of 903 occupations in the United States. Specifically, Frey and Osborne undertook the following steps:

- Provided information on work-oriented descriptors (such as worker characteristics, worker requirements, and experience requirements) and job-oriented descriptors (such as occupational requirements, workforce characteristics, and occupation-specific information) that account for tasks.
- Asked experts and researchers of automation technologies (such as machine learning and mobile robotics) to classify these occupations as either automatable or not based on their task structures.[11]
- From these, selected only 70 occupations about whose labeling the experts were highly confident.
- Projected the automatability to the rest of occupations by examining whether the classification of experts was systematically correlated with nine objective attributes of occupations that are related to the identified engineering bottlenecks (for example, manual dexterity, originality, and social perceptiveness).
- Applied a series of probabilistic models to examine the power of these bottleneck-related attributes in predicting an occupation's risk of automation.
- Applied these estimated probabilities to the occupations that were not confidently assessed by the experts.

- Divided occupations into three categories: low risk of automation (less than 30 percent), medium risk (30–70 percent), and high risk (more than 70 percent).

Merging this information with the number of people employed in each occupation in the United States, Frey and Osborne (2017) arrived at the estimate of 47 percent of jobs being at high risk of being automated—meaning, in their words, that "associated occupations are potentially automatable over some unspecified number of years, maybe a decade or two." Interestingly, they found that the risk of automation was higher for low-skilled workers and for low-wage occupations.

The main criticism of this approach is that it focuses on occupations rather than on tasks performed within an occupation. As just noted, occupations do not consist of a single task but rather a bundle of tasks, and it is tasks that are at risk of being automated, not occupations. Moreover, Frey and Osborne (2017) implicitly assumed that all workers within an occupation perform the same set of tasks. Using worker-level information on the tasks performed in an occupation reveals that a worker's task structures differ remarkably within occupations (Autor and Handel 2013).

Task-based approach
The alternative approach of Arntz, Gregory, and Zierahn (2016) to measuring job losses stemming from automation is "based on the idea that the automatability of jobs ultimately depends on the tasks which workers perform for these jobs, and how easily these tasks can be automated." Arntz , Gregory, and Zierahn (2016) used individual-level PIAAC data, which contain indicators on demographic characteristics, skills, job characteristics, and job tasks and competencies. By using individual-level data, the authors were able to incorporate possible differences in the task structure of workers within an occupation.

They estimated the relationship between workers' tasks and the risk of automation by matching the automatability indicator of Frey and Osborne (2017) to the US observations in the PIAAC database based on the occupational codes. One important drawback of this approach is that only two-digit ISCO codes are available in the PIAAC database, and thus an assignment issue arises when matching occupations with the six-digit codes of SOC. Thus the authors followed an iterative algorithm that assigned each individual in the data set the automatability with the highest probability based on this method.

This approach is less restrictive than the occupation-based approach because it allows for differences in task structures within occupations and specifically focuses on individual jobs. Moreover, the focus is on which tasks are at high risk of automation. Arntz, Gregory, and Zierahn (2016) found that the automatability of jobs is lower in jobs with high educational job requirements or jobs that require cooperation with other employees or in which people spend more time influencing others. At the other end, high-risk tasks are those related to exchanging information, selling, or using fingers and hands. These results are more in line with the literature on tasks in which routine tasks are susceptible to automation, whereas tasks related to social interaction or cognitive tasks are less likely to be automated (Acemoglu and Autor 2011; Autor and Handel 2013).

In general, the task-based approach produces estimates that are far below those presented by Frey and Osborne (2017). For example, although Frey and Osborne find that 47 percent of jobs in the United States are at high risk of being automated, Arntz, Gregory, and Zierahn (2016) find that only 9 percent have a high probability (more than 70 percent) of being automated. For OECD countries, they find that only 9 percent of jobs are at high risk of being automated.

Measuring the risk of automation: Critiques

These approaches are subject to several critiques. First, both approaches to measuring the risk of automation are based on the technical feasibility of automation and do not consider the economic desirability of adopting these technologies. Thus even though certain tasks or occupations may be technically at risk of being automated, those results should not be equated with employment losses. Adoption of these technologies will depend on the relative factor prices of capital and labor. In fact, both approaches suggest that lower-skilled, low-wage occupations are technically more at risk of being automated (mostly because they perform more routine tasks). Yet by virtue of being low-wage occupations, the price of capital will need to drop relatively more to make automation economically attractive.

Second, there is little consideration of the speed of adoption of these technologies. This is particularly relevant to developing countries. Adoption of new technologies generally requires a broad set of complementarities such as physical and human capital. In a recent publication, "The Innovation Paradox: Developing-Country Capabilities and the Unrealized Promise of Technological Catch-up," Cirera and Maloney (2017, 2) state: "If a firm (country) invests in innovation but cannot also import the necessary machines, contract trained workers and engineers, or draw on new organizational techniques, the returns to that investment will be low. In turn, the underlying conditions that impede the accumulation of any of these types of capital—such as the cost of doing business, trade regime, competitiveness framework, or capital markets, as well as those seen as particular to innovation, such as intellectual property rights protection or market failures that disincentivize the accumulation of knowledge—affect the returns and hence the quantity of innovation investment."

Other factors to consider are the legal and ethical barriers that impede or slow down the adoption of new technologies. The canonical example is that of driverless cars, which are facing legal challenges about liability in case of an accident (Bonnefon, Shariff, and Rahwan 2016; Thierer and Hagemann 2015). Also, preferences may be skewed toward the provision of services by humans rather than robots in certain businesses. For example, consumers may not resist ordering from computers or robots in fast-food restaurants, but it is not clear whether they would accept such innovations in high-end restaurants. Similarly, preferences may be skewed toward provision of services by humans in health care, nursing, and elder care, for example.

Moreover, the set of tasks performed by workers is not fixed over time, even within occupations. For example, Autor, Levy, and Murnane (2003) and Spitz-Oener (2006) found that as a response to the introduction of automation technologies, workers adjusted their work time toward tasks that were complementary to the machines. Thus it is likely that workers will change and adapt to the new technologies to avoid being unemployed.

Finally, both approaches are designed to measure the risk of automation by occupations or tasks, but generally they do not consider all of the general equilibrium effects described earlier. Neither approach considers the possibility that productivity increases could translate to higher demand in different areas of the economy, or that these technological innovations could create a whole new set of occupations and tasks that do not exist today.

Now that the caveats associated with this type of analysis have been described, the next section describes the findings of this investigation into the risks of automation in LAC economies.

Measuring the risk of automation: The LAC experience

What is the percentage of jobs at risk of automation in the LAC economies? The estimates presented here for Bolivia, Chile, and Colombia, and then all LAC countries are based on the two approaches just described—the occupation-based approach pioneered by Frey and Osborne (2017) and the task-based approach of Arntz, Gregory, and Zierahn (2016)—using the PIAAC data set for Chile. Estimates are based as well on the information available in the Skills Toward Employability and Productivity (STEP) surveys for Bolivia and Colombia, which contain worker-level information on the tasks performed at their jobs. Here an approach similar to that of Arntz, Gregory, and Zierahn (2016) is followed, with some necessary adjustments because the data sets are not strictly comparable with PIAAC.

Because no information is available for the rest of the countries in the LAC region, estimates for these countries are provided by imputing the results from the analysis of Bolivia, Chile, and Colombia. Specifically, for each country with worker-level and task-level data, the percentage of workers within an occupation that are at high risk of automation (that is, more than 70 percent) is determined. That number is then applied to the other countries using their household labor surveys. Although somewhat limited, the analysis provides a range of estimates for each country based on the methodologies and data sources available. By imputing the results from a different country, the only source of differences among countries stems from their differing occupational structures.

What follows are the results for the three countries—Chile, Colombia, and Bolivia—for which worker-level and task-level data are available. Chile's estimates are based on the PIAAC data set of OECD, and Colombia's and Bolivia's are based on the STEP surveys of the World Bank. Although the purpose of the surveys is similar—identifying the tasks and skills required in the workplace—there are some important differences in the questions asked and in the specific responses available. Therefore, the results are not strictly comparable among these countries.

Results for Chile

The findings for Chile, based on the data available from the PIACC survey produced by OECD and following closely the task-based approach developed by Arntz, Gregory, and Zierahn (2016), are in line with the results found for OECD countries. In addition, the automation risk by occupation calculated by Frey and Osborne (2017) is imputed and applied to the data for Chile. The fact that in Arntz, Gregory, and Zierahn (2016) the PIAAC data are at a two-digit level of aggregation to describe occupations, whereas the data from Frey and Osborne are disaggregated to a six-digit level, presented an assignment problem. To resolve the problem, the study team followed the approach of Arntz, Gregory, and Zierahn (2016), using an algorithm to assign the most likely risk level given the characteristics of the worker and the job.

A comparison of the task-based and occupation-based approaches reveals very different risk profiles across jobs and occupations. Most strikingly, the range of automation risk is highest when imputing the risk number from Frey and Osborne (2017), 46 percent, and lowest when applying the task-based approach, 6.5 percent.

Consistent with previous findings, the study results indicate that use of the Frey and Osborne (2017) methodology generates a bipolar distribution of automation risk with peaks close to the extremes (see figure 3.6). In other words, the occupation-based approach suggests that a significant number of jobs have a very low risk (less than 30 percent) of automation and a high number of workers have a high risk (more than 70 percent). The distribution is relatively flat and low for jobs in the middle-risk category (30–70 percent).

By contrast, the task-based approach produces a smoother distribution with a peak at the lower end of the risk spectrum, suggesting that many jobs are relatively safe from automation. Although these estimates suggest that few jobs are at high risk of being automated (less than 7 percent), there is a significant number of jobs in the middle-risk category. Workers in these types of jobs are generally performing a bundle of tasks, some of which are at risk of being automated, while other tasks are thought to be safe. Thus, although these jobs are not at high risk of disappearing, it is likely they will be significantly transformed as automation technologies become more powerful. Therefore, workers will find themselves needing to adapt to a workplace with more technology that replaces some of their tasks, and they will need the flexibility to perform the tasks complementary to the work of machines.

FIGURE 3.6   **Distribution of automatability across methodologies, Chile**

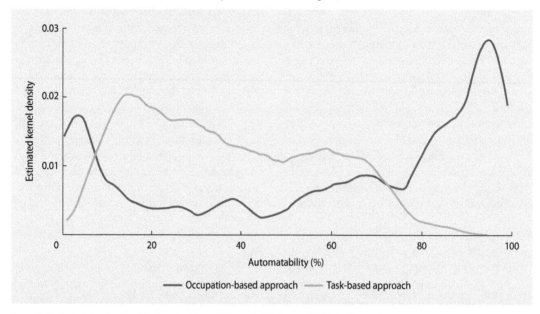

Source: Original calculations for this publication using Frey and Osborne (2017) values and PIAAC data for Chile from Organisation for Economic Co-operation and Development (https://www.oecd.org/skills/piaac/).
Note: In the occupation-based approach, Frey and Osborne values are applied to ISCO occupations in PIAAC's Chile data, using identical weights for each six-digit SOC occupation within the corresponding two-digit ISCO occupation. ISCO = International Standard Classification of Occupations; PIAAC = Programme for the International Assessment of Adult Competencies; SOC = Standard Occupational Classification.

Results for Colombia

The results for Colombia are based on the worker-level data available in the STEP surveys produced by the World Bank. Although these surveys serve the same purpose as the PIAAC surveys, there are some significant differences in the specific questions asked and, more important, in the format of the available responses. Therefore, the task-based methodology of Arntz, Gregory, and Zierahn (2016) had to be adapted to the specific format of the STEP surveys.[12]

The occupation-based approach generates a similar distribution to that of Chile and Bolivia: a bipolar distribution, with the mass concentrated in the low-risk and high-risk categories, whereas there is little mass in the middle-risk category. For Colombia, a smaller mass of employment is concentrated in the low-risk category relative to Chile and Bolivia. According to this methodology, 48 percent of jobs are at risk of being automated.

The results for Colombia using the task-based approach are very different from those for Chile and those for Bolivia. In particular, the occupation-based approach and the task-based approach yield closer results. Although this finding is not reflected in the percentage of high-risk jobs—the Frey and Osborne (2017) imputation suggests that 48 percent of jobs are at high risk, whereas the task-based approach is about half, 24.6 percent—the risk distribution profiles are not quite as dissimilar as they were for Chile (see figure 3.7).

The task-based approach using STEP data generates a distribution with a peak close to (but below) the 70 percent cutoff point. Thus it suggests that a large mass of workers are in occupations in which a significant number of the tasks they perform are at risk of being automated. The results are somewhat worrisome because the introduction of new technologies will require workers to gain the flexibility to successfully adapt to and perform the more complex tasks that are complementary to machines. As noted later in this chapter, it would be advisable for

FIGURE 3.7   Distribution of automatability across methodologies, Colombia

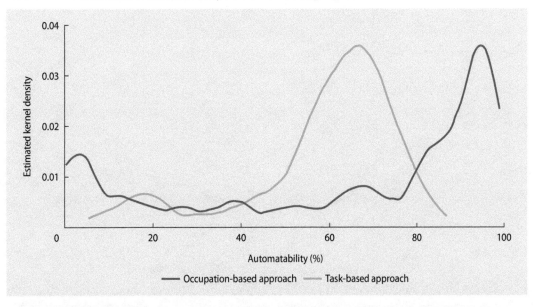

Source: Original calculations for this publication using Frey and Osborne (2017) values and data for Colombia from World Bank's STEP Skills Measurement Program (https://microdata.worldbank.org/index.php/catalog/step/about).
Note: In the occupation-based approach, Frey and Osborne values are applied to ISCO occupations in STEP data, using identical weights for each six-digit SOC occupation within the corresponding two-digit ISCO occupation. ISCO = International Standard Classification of Occupations; SOC = Standard Occupational Classification; STEP = Skills Toward Employability and Productivity.

authorities to manage these risks by investing in education and on-the-job-training programs that can help workers adapt to the new technologies and the significant changes that may be coming to their occupations.

Results for Bolivia

The results for Bolivia are based on the worker-level data available in the STEP survey produced by the World Bank. Although these surveys serve the same purpose as the PIAAC surveys, there are some significant differences in the specific questions asked and, more important, in the format of the available responses. Therefore, the task-based methodology of Arntz, Gregory, and Zierahn (2016) had to be adapted to the specific format of the STEP survey.[13] The results, however, are comparable between Colombia and Bolivia.

As it does for the other countries in the sample, the Frey and Osborne (2017) approach produces a bipolar distribution. However, in the case of Bolivia more mass is concentrated in the high-risk category. The Frey and Osborne approach yields an estimate that almost 50 percent of jobs will disappear to automation. Interestingly, the results for Bolivia are quite different from those for both Colombia and Chile. The distribution displayed in figure 3.8 shows a more uniform distribution, with a relatively small peak close to (but below) the 70 percent cutoff. Consequently, the estimate based on the task-based approach is lower than that for Colombia, 16.7 percent.

Although it is hard to pinpoint all the potential sources for the differences between Colombia and Bolivia, two factors play a major role. First, the occupational structures of the two countries are different (for example, the manufacturing sector is larger in Colombia). Second, the task structure within occupations may be different. In particular, the set of tasks performed by workers within an occupation appears to be more heterogeneous in Bolivia, involving more tasks that are difficult to automate.

FIGURE 3.8   **Distribution of automatability across methodologies, Bolivia**

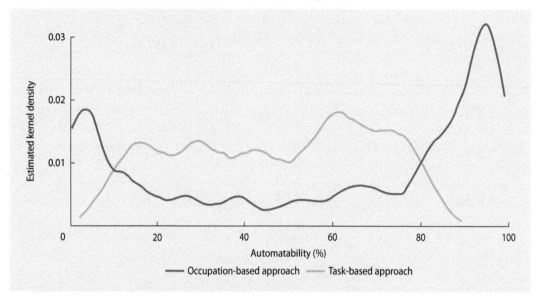

Source: Original calculations for this publication using Frey and Osborne (2017) values and data for Colombia from World Bank's STEP Skills Measurement Program (https://microdata.worldbank.org/index.php/catalog/step/about).
Note: In the occupation-based approach, Frey and Osborne values are applied to ISCO occupations in STEP data, using identical weights for each six-digit SOC occupation within the corresponding two-digit ISCO occupation. ISCO = International Standard Classification of Occupations; SOC = Standard Occupational Classification; STEP = Skills Toward Employability and Productivity.

Results for all LAC countries

This section turns to a larger sample of countries for which automation probabilities were imputed by occupation using the results for Bolivia, Chile, and Colombia.

Assessment of the number of jobs at high risk of being automated in the larger sample of countries is based on the results obtained from the estimations for Bolivia, Chile, and Colombia and the results of Frey and Osborne (2017). The estimated risk probabilities by occupation are paired with the occupational structure of each country, which is derived from the harmonized household survey data available from SEDLAC for 16 countries in the LAC region. The results identify the percentage of workers within an occupation that are at high risk of automation according to the methodologies and data sets used. Thus for each country in the sample, four different assessments are presented of the number of jobs at high risk: first, the numbers derived from Frey and Osborne's (2017) occupation-based approach; second,

imputed probabilities derived from Chile using the PIAAC data set; and third and fourth, the probabilities derived from the analysis of Bolivia and of Colombia using STEP data. For the three countries with task-related data, the numbers are based on the specific survey data (STEP and PIAAC), and, for cross-country comparability, the imputed numbers merged with the household survey data are included.

In interpreting the results, it is important to note that because the probabilities of automation are imputed by occupation, the differences across countries stem solely from the different occupational structures. So, for example, the difference between the Frey and Osborne (2017) estimates for Argentina and Uruguay are attributable to Argentina having fewer workers employed in occupations that are at high risk—according to Frey and Osborne—of being automated.

The results show some clear patterns (see figure 3.9). Clearly, the occupation-based approach consistently produces the highest

FIGURE 3.9   **Risk of automation by LAC country, based on four methodologies**

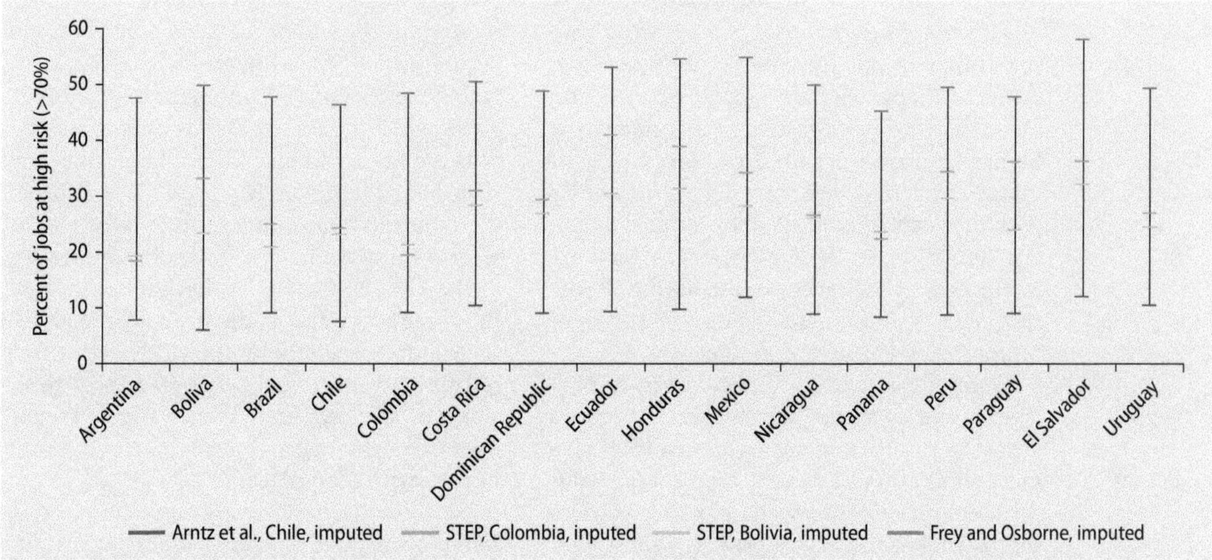

Sources: Original calculations for this publication using 2016 PIAAC data from Organisation for Economic Co-operation and Development (https://www.oecd.org
/skills/piaac/); data for Colombia and Bolivia from World Bank's STEP Skills Measurement Program (https://microdata.worldbank.org/index.php/catalog/step/about);
Socio-Economic Database for Latin America and the Caribbean (SEDLAC) household surveys, CEDLAS and World Bank (https://datacatalog.worldbank.org/dataset
/socio-economic-database-latin-america-and-caribbean).
Note: Study team calculations follow the methodology of Frey and Osborne (2017) and Arntz, Gregory, and Zierahn (2016). Numbers indicate the percentage of jobs at high risk of
being automated, using a cutoff of 70 percent as is standard in the literature. CEDLAS = Center for Distributive, Labor and Social Studies; LAC = Latin America and the Caribbean;
STEP = Skills Toward Employability and Productivity.

estimates, and thus could be interpreted as
an upper bound. In the sample, the estimates
across countries range from a minimum of
45.1 percent for Panama to 58 percent for
El Salvador; the average for the region is
50 percent. Ecuador, Honduras, Mexico,
and El Salvador seem to have more workers
employed in occupations that are more likely
to be automated. At the other end, countries
such as Argentina, Chile, and Panama seem
to have slightly fewer jobs at risk.

Use of the probabilities derived from the
PIAAC data set for Chile results in the lowest
estimates of jobs at risk, and so can be interpreted as the lower bound. The estimates
range from a low of 6 percent for Bolivia
to a high of 12 percent for El Salvador; the
average for the region is 9.2 percent. Once
again, Argentina and Chile are the countries
facing below-average risk, whereas Ecuador,
Mexico, El Salvador, and Uruguay display
higher numbers of jobs at risk.

Applying the estimates using the
Colombia STEP data set produces a range

that is wider than those for the previous
two methodologies. The results indicate
that Argentina, at 18.3 percent, faces the
least number of jobs, while Ecuador has the
highest, with over 40 percent of the workforce at high risk. The average for the region
using this methodology is 29.8 percent.
Argentina, Chile, and Colombia appear to
be significantly below the regional average,
whereas Ecuador, Honduras, Mexico, Peru,
Paraguay, and El Salvador are highest in the
risk rankings.

Finally, use of the numbers from the
Bolivia STEP survey produces a range that
is not as wide as that using the Colombia
numbers. Once again Argentina, at 19.2
percent, has the least number of jobs at risk,
whereas El Salvador accounts for the maximum, 32.2 percent. The regional average
is 25.8 percent. The results indicate that
Argentina, Brazil, and Colombia have the
least number of jobs at risk, and Ecuador,
Honduras, and El Salvador have the highest
number of jobs at risk.

Clearly, the methodological approach used to assess how many jobs are at risk of automation is of vital importance, and the choice is not innocuous. The occupation-based approach developed by Frey and Osborne (2017) consistently produces the highest probabilities, and the range of estimates is narrow, not varying significantly with the occupational structure of each country. According to these estimates, which are interpreted as an upper bound, about 50 percent of jobs in the LAC region are at risk of disappearing because of automation.

Beyond the methodological approach, it is apparent that the data source matters as well. Use of different surveys, even if all estimate skills and tasks in the workforce, yields different estimates as well. The PIAAC data set for Chile consistently produces the lowest estimates for each country, and once again the range of estimates is very narrow, virtually unaffected by the occupation structure of countries. Thus the results based on this methodology and data source are interpreted as the lower bound. In general, these results suggest that the fear of mass technological unemployment are wildly overblown because only 10 percent of jobs could be at risk.

Data from the STEP surveys, which are comparable, yield estimates that are for the most part similar when comparing the numbers from the Bolivia analysis or the Colombia analysis. The exceptions are Bolivia, Ecuador, and Paraguay, where the estimates differ by more than 10 percentage points.

However, cutting across methodologies and data sources, some patterns emerge. For example, some of the more advanced countries in the region, such as Argentina and Chile, consistently display the lowest estimated number of jobs at risk. At the other end, countries such as Ecuador, Honduras, and El Salvador, some of the least developed countries in the region, consistently display a larger number of jobs at risk. It appears, then, that higher levels of development are associated with an occupational structure in which tasks are more complex or more difficult to automate and therefore result in fewer jobs being at risk. This finding should be of great concern to the less developed countries in the region, which, according to the estimates, are facing higher risks of automation.

Several patterns also cut across the empirical analysis. First, the occupation-based approach produces a bipolar distribution that concentrates the mass of workers in the low-risk category and mostly in the high-risk category. Differences among the three countries at the heart of the analysis are driven solely by their different occupational structures. Chile has the lowest share of workers at risk with 46.3 percent, then Colombia with 48.3 percent, and finally Bolivia with 49.7 percent.

Second, the risk of automation is negatively correlated with both education and income (see figure 3.10, panels a and b). The visual results are confirmed by the statistical analysis. Workers who are less educated and earn less tend to work in occupations that involve more manual and routine tasks—the very tasks associated with a high degree of automation. On the other hand, workers who are more educated tend to work in occupations that have higher intensity of cognitive/analytical tasks, as well as complex social interactions such as teamwork, negotiation, and creative problem solving.

Finally, although the task-based approach produces a much smaller number of jobs at high risk of being automated, all three countries display a significant mass of workers who are close to the cutoff. This finding suggests that although the jobs may not be at risk of disappearing, they will be highly susceptible to the introduction of new technologies. In other words, there are many workers whose workday involves a lot of tasks that will be automatable in the near future. Therefore, these workers will need to adapt soon to the new technologies and shift their task load toward the more dexterous, complex, and cognitive tasks. This may require additional skills and capabilities from workers.

FIGURE 3.10   **Automation risk by selected characteristics, LAC region**

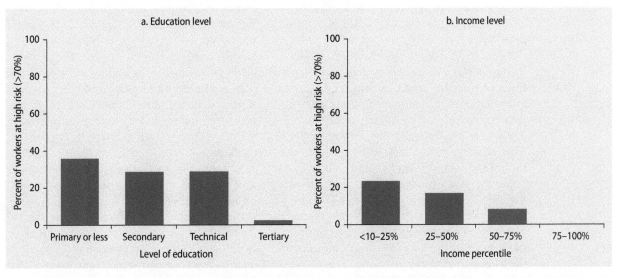

Sources: Original calculations for this publication using 2016 PIAAC data from Organisation for Economic Co-operation and Development (https://www.oecd.org/skills/piaac/); data for Colombia and Bolivia from World Bank's STEP Skills Measurement Program (https://microdata.worldbank.org/index.php/catalog/step/about); Socio-Economic Database for Latin America and the Caribbean (SEDLAC) household surveys, CEDLAS and World Bank (https://datacatalog.worldbank.org/dataset/socio-economic-database-latin-america-and-caribbean). CEDLAS = Center for Distributive, Labor and Social Studies; LAC = Latin America and the Caribbean; STEP = Skills Toward Employability and Productivity.

Looking into the future: Digital platforms and the nature of work

The future may bring the emergence of another potential disruption in labor markets: the rise of digital platforms as a new avenue for workers to supply labor. For most technological innovations, these platforms may present significant opportunities, but effectively benefiting from them may also present significant challenges.

On the positive side, digital platforms reduce the cost of entry for entrepreneurs and expand access to large markets. With only a smartphone and access to the internet, any entrepreneur can now engage with local, regional, and even global markets. In turn, successful businesses can scale up quickly and foster job creation. This development may be particularly important and relevant for rural communities where employment outside agricultural activities may be limited. An example of the huge opportunities for rural development is the "Taobao villages" experience in China. On the Taobao.com

Marketplace, many clusters of rural e-shops have emerged. These entrepreneurs produce goods, agricultural products, and handicrafts based on their niche competencies. It is estimated that Taobao villages have created more than 1.3 million jobs in rural communities (World Bank 2019, 39).

Digital platforms not only provide benefits for entrepreneurs selling products online, but also expand market access for professionals and service providers. Workers can participate in multiple online platforms for a relatively low entry cost and freelance, reaching millions of customers. This is a huge opportunity for a region such as Latin America and the Caribbean, where most countries share a language and have similar cultural and institutional backgrounds that can facilitate trade in professional services.

From the perspectives of consumers, there are also many potential benefits. For one thing, greater competition among entrepreneurs can result in lower prices. For another, consumers can now access a better variety and quality of products and services.

Apparently, consumers trust these platforms because they can rely on brand certification and consumer reviews to make informed decisions.

One of the major opportunities provided by digital platforms is expansion of the labor supply, thereby contributing to regional growth. Although data are limited, particularly for developing countries, most workers in advanced nations use digital platforms to earn secondary income. Workers have the flexibility and autonomy to set their own hours according to their needs and the schedules of their main occupations. This flexibility and autonomy may be particularly important for women who may be out of the labor force or have limited hours because of their home care duties.

In the context of the LAC region, another potential benefit of digital platforms is that transactions are conducted digitally and thus create an electronic record. This would allow—in principle—for the taxation of these transactions, many of which occur today on the informal side of the economy, thereby escaping taxation. This issue should not be undervalued because LAC economies are notoriously fiscally constrained, and changes in the labor market may affect the sustainability of the traditional social insurance system—an issue discussed shortly in more detail.

For all the potential benefits offered by digital platforms, they present policy makers with significant challenges. Obviously, the expansion of digital commerce requires reliable and affordable internet connectivity and high penetration of smartphones. Therefore, success in digital commerce depends on countries investing in and expanding their telecommunications infrastructure—and especially in rural communities if countries would like to replicate the success of Taobao villages.

Another challenge is setting up a regulatory framework that establishes clear and fair rules for all participants. Among several issues is the need for clear rules on the ownership of data and privacy rules for both consumers and providers on these platforms.

Also important are minimum quality standards and safety regulations. Moreover, policy makers should establish the legal framework for taxation of transactions within their country's border, but also for cross-border taxation and liability issues. These are all examples of the regulatory infrastructure that needs to be in place to foster the inclusive growth of digital platforms while protecting all participants in these markets.

Finally, the greater supply of labor available through digital platforms has opened an important debate on whether to consider these workers as employees of the digital platform or as independent contractors or freelancers. Moreover, the rise of these alternative forms of labor supply may threaten the sustainability of the traditional social insurance model. As more and more workers—both skilled and unskilled—participate in these platforms, the social insurance mechanism that relies on employer-employee contributions to finance social protection will slowly degrade. From the perspective of the LAC region, which already has high levels of informality in the labor market, this is particularly worrisome. Policy makers in the region must think creatively about alternative social insurance models that do not rely on financing and benefits attached to formal employer–employee relationships. In other words, policy makers need to both define the level of social protection and insurance that will be provided to citizens regardless of their labor status and relationship (that is, employee, contractor, or freelance) and find alternative financing mechanisms that do not depend on the employee–employer relationship.

Conclusions and policy implications

In general, this analysis has found that the risk of mass technological unemployment is low for the LAC economies. In addition, the slow adoption rate for these technologies suggests that massive changes in the workplace are not likely to occur in the next decade. However, this analysis also suggests that many jobs will be affected and transformed by the emergence of these technologies. And although these jobs may not disappear completely, many of the tasks performed by humans today will likely be performed by machines in the future. Workers will be interacting with more machines and increasingly complex technologies. Therefore, they will need the capabilities and skills to adjust to these new demands.

There is a growing consensus that the demand for skills in the labor market is changing. These changes have been under way over the last two decades in advanced economies, and because technology is being adopted in developing countries, these changes are beginning to occur there as well. Reinforcing these changes are new technologies that are emerging and threatening to replace humans, mostly in the simpler, more routine tasks they perform at work.

According to the *World Development Report 2016: Digital Dividends*, the skills required for the modern economy go beyond the foundational cognitive skills such as basic literacy and numeracy. Some of the most valued skills that also have a low risk of automation are the nonroutine, higher-order ones. These skills are related to the ability to understand complex concepts, learn from experience, adapt to new situations, and more generally solve problems by using critical thinking. The need for nonroutine interpersonal, socioemotional skills is also on the rise. As stated in the *World Development Report 2016*,

"Socioemotional skills (also called soft or noncognitive skills) encompass a broad range of malleable skills, behaviors, attitudes, and personality traits that enable individuals to navigate interpersonal and social situations effectively. These include grit or the perseverance to finish a job or achieve a long-term goal, working in teams, punctuality, organization, commitment, creativity, and honesty" (World Bank 2016, 213).

As revealed in this analysis and consistent with the literature, education continues to be the best asset to insure against the risks of automation. The low-paid and uneducated workers performing the simpler, more routine tasks are most at risk of being replaced by machines. By virtue of being in lower-paid occupations, such tasks may in the short run be less likely to be automated because the prices of robots and automation technologies need to drop further for adoption to be economically desirable. However, in the medium and long term these tasks are at high risk of being fully automated.

Thus investing in the human capital of the workforce should be a priority for policy makers. Investing in early childhood education reaps the highest return on investments, and the advantages grow over time because learning and skill development are cumulative. In fact, Engle et al. (2011) find that every additional US$1 invested in quality early childhood education programs yields a return of US$6–$17. When quality and access are ensured, investments in early childhood education also increase equity, and there are several examples of successful programs in the LAC region. Cash transfers that increase the take-up of early childhood education programs have fostered language development in Ecuador and Mexico. Chile's Crece Contigo program integrates the health, education, welfare, and protection services available as of the first prenatal visit of the mother.

Although the LAC region has made substantial progress in improving access to secondary education, the quality of education continues to lag that of advanced nations and developing country peers in East Asia. Thus the focus should be on increasing the quality of secondary education and preparing students for further education, whether in vocational trade schools or university.

Meanwhile, the demand for higher-order nonroutine cognitive skills is increasing. Tertiary education is therefore becoming more important for the future of work. Not only does it impart the technical skills required for certain occupations, but it also fosters development of the complex problem-solving, critical thinking, and advanced communications skills that are transferable across jobs and occupations. Tertiary education also builds the transferable sociobehavioral skills—such as teamwork, resilience, and self-confidence—that have also seen higher demand in the labor market. Policy makers should focus on how to improve the access to and quality of tertiary systems (both trade schools and universities) in order to improve the capabilities of the future workforce. A deep analysis of the tertiary system in the LAC region can be found in the report *At a Crossroads: Higher Education in Latin America and the Caribbean* by Ferreyra et al. (2017).

Finally, what may become more important as new automation technologies are adopted in LAC countries is adult learning. Although the time frame for the adoption of technology is unclear, it is possible that transformations in the workplace will happen midcareer for many workers, and they will need to adapt, particularly by changing the set of tasks performed at work. Governments should have programs that help workers upskill and retrain for the new jobs and minimize their adjustment costs. Meanwhile, the design of adult learning programs should take into account the constraints often facing adults in terms of time, financial resources, and competing demands. Meanwhile, behavioral and neuroscience research has discovered that the adult brain learns differently.

The success of these types of programs already in the region is mixed. Argentina's Entra21 program is providing adult skills training and internships resulting in 40 percent higher earnings for its participants (J-PAL 2017). In Peru, a female entrepreneurship program did not generate significant effects on employment. Similarly, in the Dominican Republic the Juventud y Empleo program did not increase employment, although it improved noncognitive skills and job formality. The evidence suggests that adult learning programs are most successful when they are tied to employment opportunities. Thus programs that include apprenticeships and internships in partnership with the private sector will generally

have more lasting and significant effects. For example, Colombia's Jovenes en Acción program, which combines learning with on-the-job training, has shown that the probability of formal employment and earnings increases in the short term, and it has seen the benefits sustained over time.

Notes

1. See, among others, Brynjolfsson and McAfee (2014); McKinsey Global Institute (2017); World Bank (2016, 2019); World Economic Forum (2018).
2. The recent phenomenon of labor market polarization has been documented by Autor, Katz, and Kearney (2008) and Autor and Dorn (2013) for the United States, and Goos and Manning (2007) for the United Kingdom. Job polarization has also been documented for Germany (Dustmann, Ludsteck, and Schönberg 2009; Spitz-Oener 2006), and there are indications it is pervasive in European countries (Goos, Manning, and Salomons 2009; Michaels, Natraj, and Van Reenen 2013).
3. The Skills Toward Employment and Productivity (STEP) survey is not available for the LAC region.
4. Using the STEP survey, Dicarlo et al. (2016) show that the task content in the United States and developing economies is generally similar for high-skilled occupations, while remarkably different for routine-based occupations.
5. Croatia, Czech Republic, Estonia, Hungary, Latvia, Lithuania, Poland, Romania, Slovakia, and Slovenia.
6. Many of the surveys in the region are urban and thus underrepresent the agriculture sector.
7. Moore's Law asserts that computer power doubles every 18 months.
8. If a demand for a product is inelastic, then the increase in quantity demanded does not fully compensate for the fall in prices and revenues. If demand is elastic, the increase in demand is proportionally higher than the fall in prices, revenues increase, and more workers will be hired to produce more units.
9. General-purpose technologies are defined as "deep new ideas or techniques that have the potential for important impacts on many sectors of the economy" (Wright 2000).

10. Specialists who help website providers secure high rankings on the results pages of search engines such as Google.

11. Specifically, experts were asked, "Can the tasks of this job be sufficiently specified conditional on the availability of big data, to be performed by state-of-the-art computer-controlled equipment?" (Frey and Osborne 2017).

12. For technical details, see Beylis and Cuevas (2019).

13. For technical details, refer to Beylis and Cuevas (2019).

References

Acemoglu, D., and D. Autor. 2011. "Skills, Tasks and Technologies: Implications for Employment and Earnings." *Handbook of Labor Economics* 4: 1043–171.

Aedo, C., J. Hentschel, J. Luque, and M. Moreno. 2013. "From Occupations to Embedded Skills: A Cross-Country Comparison." Policy Research Working Paper 6560, World Bank, Washington, DC.

Arntz, M., T. Gregory, and U. Zierahn. 2016. "The Risk of Automation for Jobs in OECD Countries: A Comparative Analysis." OECD Social, Employment, and Migration Working Paper 189, Organisation for Economic Co-operation and Development, Paris.

Artuc, E., L. Christiaensen, and H. Winkler. 2019. "Does Automation in Rich Countries Hurt Developing Ones? Evidence from US and Mexico." Policy Research Working Paper 8741, World Bank, Washington, DC.

Autor, D. 2014. "Skills, Education, and the Rise of Earnings Inequality among the 'Other 99 Percent.'" *Science* 344 (6186): 843–51.

Autor, D. 2015. "Polanyi's Paradox and the Shape of Employment Growth." In *Reevaluating Labor Market Dynamics,* Economic Policy Proceedings, 129–77. Kansas City, MO: Federal Reserve Bank of Kansas City.

Autor, D., and D. Dorn. 2009. "Inequality and Specialization: The Growth of Low-Skill Service Jobs in the United States." NBER Working Paper 15150, National Bureau of Economic Research, Cambridge, MA.

Autor, D., and D. Dorn. 2013. "The Growth of Low Skill Service Jobs and the Polarization of the US Labor Market." *American Economic Review* 103 (5): 1553–97.

Autor, D. H., and M. J. Handel. 2013. "Putting Tasks to the Test: Human Capital, Job Tasks, and Wages." *Journal of Labor Economics* 31 (S1): S59–S96.

Autor, D. H., L. F. Katz, and M. S. Kearney. 2006. "The Polarization of the U.S. Labor Market." *American Economic Review* 96: 1553–97.

Autor, D. H., L. F. Katz, and M. S. Kearney. 2008. "Trends in US Wage Inequality: Revising the Revisionists." *Review of Economics and Statistics* 90 (2): 300–23.

Autor, D. H., F. Levy, and R. J. Murnane. 2003. "The Skill Content of Recent Technological Change: An Empirical Exploration." *Quarterly Journal of Economics* 118 (4): 1279–333.

Basker, E. 2015. "Change at the Checkout: Tracing the Impact of a Process Innovation." *Journal of Industrial Economics* 63 (2): 339–70.

Bessen, J. E. 2016. "How Computer Automation Affects Occupations: Technology, Jobs, and Skills." Law and Economics Research Paper 15–49, Boston University School of Law.

Beylis, Guillermo, and Maria Ignacia Paz Cuevas de Saint Pierre. 2020. "Measuring Job Loss Risk to Automation in LAC: Methods and Data Sources." Background technical paper, World Bank, Washington, DC.

Bolt, J., R. Inklaar, H. de Jong, and J. Luiten van Zanden. 2018. "Rebasing 'Maddison': New Income Comparisons and the Shape of Long-run Economic Development." Maddison Project Working Paper 10, Groningen Growth and Development Centre (GGDC), Groningen, The Netherlands.

Bonnefon, J. F., A. Shariff, and I. Rahwan. 2016. "The Social Dilemma of Autonomous Vehicles." *Science* 352 (6293): 1573–76.

Brynjolfsson, E., and A. McAfee. 2014. *The Second Machine Age: Work, Progress, and Prosperity in a Time of Brilliant Technologies.* New York: Norton.

Cirera, X. and W. F. Maloney. 2017. *The Innovation Paradox: Developing-Country Capabilities and the Unrealized Promise of Technological Catch-Up.* Washington, DC: World Bank.

Dicarlo, E., S. Lo Bello, S. Monroy-Taborda, A. M. Oviedo, M. L. Sanchez Puerta, and I. V. Santos. 2016. "The Skill Content of Occupations across Low and Middle Income Countries: Evidence from Harmonized Data." IZA DP7 (102240).

Duernecker, G., and B. Herrendorf. 2017. "Structural Transformation of Occupation

Employment." https://economicdynamics.org /meetpapers/2017/paper_1239.pdf.

Dustmann, C., J. Ludsteck, and U. Schönberg. 2009. "Revisiting the German Wage Structure." *Quarterly Journal of Economics* 124 (2): 843–81.

Eden, M., and P. Gaggl. 2015. "On the Welfare Implications of Automation." Policy Research Working Paper 7487, World Bank, Washington, DC.

Engle, P. L., L. C. H. Fernald, H. Alderman, J. R. Behrman, C. O'Gara, A. Yousafzai, M. Cabral de Mello, et al. 2011. "Strategies for Reducing Inequalities and Improving Developmental Outcomes for Young Children in Low-Income and Middle-Income Countries." *Lancet* 378 (9799): 1339–53.

Ferreyra, M., C. Avitabile, J. Botero Álvarez, F. Haimovich Paz, and S. Urzúa. 2017. *At a Crossroads: Higher Education in Latin America and the Caribbean.* Washington, DC: World Bank.

Frey, C. B., and M. A. Osborne. 2017. "The Future of Employment: How Susceptible Are Jobs to Computerisation?" *Technological Forecasting and Social Change* 114 (January): 254–80.

Goos, M., and A. Manning. 2007. "Lousy and Lovely Jobs: The Rising Polarization of Work in Britain." *Review of Economics and Statistics* 89 (1): 118–33.

Goos, M., A. Manning, and A. Salomons. 2009. "Job Polarization in Europe." *American Economic Review* 99 (2): 58–63.

Goos, M., A. Manning, and A. Salomons. 2014. "Explaining Job Polarization: Routine-Biased Technological Change and Offshoring." American Economic Review, 104 (8): 2509-26.

Hardy, W., R. Keister, and P. Lewandowski. 2016. "Technology or Upskilling? Trends in the Task Composition of Jobs in Central and Eastern Europe." HKUST IEMS Working Paper No. 2016–40, BS Working Paper Series, Institute of Structural Research (IBS), Warsaw, Poland.

Hardy, W., R. Keister, and P. Lewandowski. 2018. "Educational Upgrading, Structural Change and the Task Composition of Jobs in Europe." *Economics of Transition* 26 (2): 201–31.

J-PAL (Abdul Latif Jameel Poverty Action Lab). 2017. "Skills Training Programmes." Cambridge, MA, August.

Maloney, W. F., and C. Molina. 2016. "Are Automation and Trade Polarizing Developing Country Labor Markets, Too?" World Bank, Washington, DC.

McKinley, R.A., ed. 1958. *The City of Leicester: A History of the County of Leicester.* Vol 4. Victoria County History Series. Martlesham, Suffolk, UK: Boydell and Brewer.

McKinsey Global Institute. 2017. "Jobs lost, Jobs Gained: Workforce Transitions in a Time of Automation." December.

Messina, J., A. M. Oviedo, and G. Pica. 2016. "Job Polarization in Latin America." Unpublished paper. World Bank, Washington, DC.

Michaels, G., A. Natraj, and J. Van Reenen. 2013. "Has ICT Polarized Skill Demand? Evidence from Eleven Countries over 25 Years." *Review of Economics and Statistics* 96 (1): 60–77.

Minnesota Population Center. 2019. Integrated Public Use Microdata Series, International: Version 7.2 (data set). IPUMS, Minneapolis, MN. https://doi.org/10.18128/D020.V7.2.

Spitz-Oener, A. 2006. "Technical Change, Job Tasks, and Rising Educational Demands: Looking Outside the Wage Structure." *Journal of Labor Economics* 24 (2): 235–70.

Susskind, Daniel, and Richard Susskind. 2015. *Professions: How Technology Will Transform the Work of Human Experts.* Oxford, UK: Oxford University Press.

Thierer, A., and R. Hagemann. 2015. "Removing Roadblocks to Intelligent Vehicles and Driverless Cars." *Wake Forest Journal of Law and Policy* 5: 339.

World Bank. 2016. *World Development Report 2016: Digital Dividends.* Washington, DC: World Bank.

World Bank. 2019. *World Development Report 2019: The Nature of Work.* Washington, DC: World Bank.

World Economic Forum. 2018. *The Future of Jobs Report 2018.* Cologny, Switzerland.

Wright, Gavin. 2000. "Review of Helpman (1998)." *Journal of Economic Literature* 38 (March): 161–62.

Zeng Kunhua. 1973. *Zhongguo tie lu shi [The History of Chinese Railway Development].* Vol. 1. Taipei, Taiwan, China: Wenhai Press.

Conclusions | 4

The Latin America and the Caribbean (LAC) region is facing important challenges. After a decade of rapid growth and strong improvements in social indicators, growth has stalled, and external conditions do not appear to be favorable, at least in the short and medium term. Trade flows have slowed amid elevated tensions, foreign direct investment (FDI) has fallen off, financing conditions are tightening, and all of this is happening in the context of vulnerable fiscal conditions for governments in the region. Commodity prices, which helped fuel growth during the so-called Golden Decade (2003–13), are expected to remain flat in the short and medium term. The region therefore needs to find internal sources of growth, suggesting that priority should be given to a reform agenda focused on productivity growth.

At the same time, the world is facing the huge opportunities and challenges that arise with the new technologies of the Fourth Industrial Revolution. Of particular concern to policy makers and workers is the emergence of automation technologies that threaten to destroy a substantial number of jobs and risk massive unemployment. Although this report finds that

mass "technological unemployment"—as these concerns are now labeled—is unlikely, the labor market is undergoing a major transformation, and government action is urgently needed to prepare the workforce for the future.

Structural transformation: Past and future

In the LAC region, structural transformation has contributed negatively to productivity growth. The relative share of employment in services—the sector with the lowest rate of productivity growth—has significantly increased. In fact, this analysis finds that, consistent with the findings of Rodrik (2016), the structural transformation path followed by LAC countries is systematically different from the path followed in the past by what are today developed countries. Specifically, the region is entering the deindustrialization phase earlier (at lower levels of gross domestic product per capita) and achieving lower peaks of industrial shares relative to developed countries. This "premature deindustrialization" is worrisome because in most countries the industrial sector has the highest level of labor productivity and the highest rate of productivity growth. When premature deindustrialization occurs, labor moves from the industrial sector to the lower productivity growth sectors, usually services, reducing overall productivity (so-called Baumol's disease), with negative consequences for real income growth and standards of living.

From this analysis of the structural transformation process of nine LAC economies with different development levels, three features stand out. The first is the substantial heterogeneity across the countries in the sample. The more developed economies—Argentina and Chile—have been deindustrializing for decades. Brazil, Colombia, and Mexico display stagnant or slight increases in their industrial employment shares. The least developed country in the sample, Bolivia, is still in the industrialization phase of development. Second, the deindustrialization process is more pronounced in terms of employment shares than in value-added shares. Similar to the experience of the United States, this feature is indicative of the rapid labor productivity growth in this sector. Third, premature deindustrialization does not necessarily imply a contraction of the industrial sector; the absolute number of jobs in that sector—as opposed to the share of jobs—has been fairly stable or even growing in most LAC economies.

What are the implications of the changes in industrialization for the future? The emergence of new technologies suggests that opportunities for further industrialization (or reindustrialization) are likely to be limited in many developing countries. Requirements in terms of complementary infrastructure and skills will increase, and global value chains are expected to shorten, reducing opportunities for entry. To stay competitive, firms will need to adopt many of these new technologies, which tend to be labor-saving. Overall, the industrial sector will likely continue to contribute positively to aggregate productivity growth and value added, but not as much to job creation, especially for unskilled labor.

This is not to say that policy makers should now ignore the industrial sector. Evidence from this analysis clearly shows that significant distortions remain in the sector. This is reflected in a skewed firm size distribution in which many firms in the LAC region remain small relative to what is observed for the United States. Policies that foster international competition within the region and globally should receive priority. Also needed are changes in the size-dependent policies that are disincentivizing the growth of firms and incentivizing informality. Policy makers should encourage adoption of technology, improve the business environment, and provide the telecommunications, transport, and logistics infrastructure required for firms to grow. Governments should also continue to invest in human capital development, with a specific focus on the technical and socioemotional skills that will be demanded by the modern industrial sector.

That said, the region is confronting a future in which the services sector will continue to grow and be the main source of job creation. Meanwhile, the region will have to remedy lack of understanding about the complex role of the services sector in productivity, value added, and job creation. At the aggregate level, the services sector displays lower productivity growth than the industrial sector. Yet the sector is composed of a very diverse set of subsectors that differ significantly in their productivity levels and growth rates, and even in their use of skilled labor. In many countries, some service subsectors—such as telecommunications, finance, and logistics—are more productive and skill-intensive than manufacturing and are increasingly sharing pro-development characteristics that were once thought to be unique to manufacturing. The rapid advances in information and communications technology (ICT) have enabled the emergence of services sectors that are no longer limited by market size because more and more services can be digitally stored, codified, and easily traded (Ghani and Kharas 2010). Meanwhile, the deregulation of services markets has been accompanied by large inflows of FDI. Therefore, certain service subsectors are looking more and more like the industrial sector, with exposure to trade and inflows of FDI, allowing for greater competition, technology diffusion, and the benefits of scale.

Many of these services are emerging as key inputs into industrial and agricultural processes, with numerous forward linkages to other sectors and huge potential to improve aggregate productivity. In fact, new evidence is pointing to a "servicification" of the manufacturing sector—that is, manufacturing is increasing the share of services used in the production process (embodied services), as well as bundling more sales and after-sales services in the sales of goods (embedded services). Reducing distortions in the intermediate market for services could have an important impact on the size of the industrial sector. Calculations indicate that the industrial sector could increase by 2–3.5 percentage points if distortions in the services market were reduced to their historical minimum.

Meanwhile, it will be increasingly relevant to formulate value chain policies in addition to sector-specific policies—that is, policy makers may have a larger impact on aggregate productivity by understanding how sectors interact with each other rather than by studying isolated sectors (the traditional approach). It is also important to recognize that the scale-up of key backbone services may be limited not only by sector-specific distortions that prevent competition and innovation from occurring at a rapid pace, but also by the availability of skilled workers because these sectors are highly skill-intensive.

Looking forward

Looking forward, the LAC region should develop a productivity agenda with a special focus on the services sector. Already the largest employer in the region with over 60 percent of the workforce, the services sector is expected to grow even more and

play an increasingly critical role as provider of inputs to the larger economy. In short, a comprehensive set of policies oriented to the services sector is needed.

Policy makers should give priority to investing in data gathering and analysis of services sector firms in view of the lack of data for the sector. Understanding the specific issues of the sector regarding firm size distribution, dynamics, barriers to entry, lack of competition, and restrictions to trade is key to formulating policies that can unleash productivity growth in this sector.

Fostering competition and streamlining regulations in the services sector are important as well. Governments could incorporate trade in services as part of regional integration agreements and work toward establishing common licensing and certifications so workers and firms can operate throughout the region. With the emergence of digital platforms that allow workers to supply labor from a distance and across borders, establishing common regional regulatory frameworks could unleash important productivity gains across the region and spur the creation of new entrepreneurial activities and new jobs.

As for the future of work, three major economic forces are changing the nature of work and the demand for skills. First, structural transformation and the premature deindustrialization process described in this report imply that job creation in the future will be concentrated in the services sector. Second, accompanying the shift in economic structure is a transformation of the occupational structure within broad economic sectors. Service occupations—those that produce intangible value added—are rising in all sectors, implying a huge shift in the demand for skills in the labor market. Third, because the simpler, more routine tasks will be automated and performed by machines, workers will need to adapt and perform a different set of tasks in the workplace. Consistent with the empirical evidence from other countries, in the LAC region during the 2001–13 time frame of this analysis there has been a decline in the demand for routine manual tasks and a rise in the demand for nonroutine tasks—both cognitive/analytical (such as critical thinking, creativity, and problem-solving) as well as interpersonal (such as teamwork, negotiation, managing).

Based on analysis of the potential number of jobs at high risk of being automated in the region, it appears that fears of mass technological unemployment are largely unfounded. Estimates vary widely, however, depending on the methodology used. Nevertheless, many occupations will be affected and transformed by the emerging technologies. Although the overall number of jobs many not fall dramatically, many of the tasks being performed by humans today will likely be performed by machines in the future. Workers will interact with more machines and will be expected to understand increasingly complex technologies. Therefore, future jobs and tasks will require different and higher-order capabilities and skills.

Both the *World Development Report 2019: The Changing Nature of Work* (World Bank 2019) and this analysis conclude that education offers the best insurance against the risks of automation. Low-paid and uneducated workers are performing the simpler, more routine tasks, and so they are at highest risk of eventually being replaced by machines. These results point to a clear conclusion: investing in the human capital of the workforce should be a priority for policy makers. While investing in early childhood education generates the highest return on investment (World Bank 2019), there is room to improve in every dimension of the educational system.

What may become more important as new automation technologies are adopted in LAC countries are adult learning and retraining programs. It is possible that transformations in the workplace will happen midcareer for many workers. They will then need to adapt and adjust, particularly by changing the set of tasks performed at work. To minimize the adjustment costs borne by workers, governments should support programs that help workers upskill and retrain for these new jobs and tasks.

The emergence of digital platforms is another possible disruption of labor markets. On the positive side, digital platforms can significantly expand access to new markets, creating opportunities for entrepreneurs, which in turn can create new jobs. Consumers will gain access to a wider variety of products, to better quality products, and to lower prices through enhanced competition. Workers, especially women, may find that such platforms provide autonomy and flexibility they need for their needs and limitations.

Yet for these benefits to fully materialize, several regulatory and infrastructure obstacles need to be overcome. Clearly, access to affordable and reliable broadband service is a prerequisite for the success of digital platforms. Logistics infrastructure is also a must to enable efficient and affordable transportation of goods within and across countries. A regulatory framework that establishes clear and fair rules on privacy, ownership of data, safety, and minimum quality standards is also necessary.

Also arising from the findings of this analysis is an important concern: the sustainability of the traditional social protection models. The growth of employment in the services sector stemming from structural transformation and the emergence of new technologies that foster alternative working arrangements such as independent contractors and self-employment have important implications for that model. Looking into the future, it appears that less and less labor will be supplied through the traditional employer–employee relationship. For a region that already struggles with very high labor market informality, these trends pose a serious challenge to the traditional social protection model that is financed through employer-employee contributions.

Policy makers in the region must think creatively, then, about alternative social insurance models that do not rely on financing and benefits attached to formal employer–employee relationships. In other words, policy makers need to define the level of social protection and insurance that will be provided to citizens regardless of their labor status and relationship (employee, contractor, freelance) and find alternative financing mechanisms that do not depend on the employee–employer relationship. Although there are no clear and obvious solutions, the region's policy makers must begin to tackle this issue with urgency and creativity.

References

Ghani, E., and H. Kharas. 2010. "The Service Revolution." Brief 54595, World Bank, Washington, DC.

Rodrik, D. 2016. "Premature Deindustrialization." *Journal of Economic Growth* 21 (1): 1–33.

World Bank. 2019. *World Development Report 2019: The Changing Nature of Work*. Washington, DC: World Bank.